ALSO BY JUDITH VIORST

POEMS

CHILDREN'S BOOKS

OTHER

Alexander and the Wonderful, Marvelous, Excellent, Terrific Ninety Days

*An Almost Completely Honest Account of What Happened
to Our Family When Our Youngest Son, His Wife,
Their Baby, Their Toddler, and Their Five-Year-Old
Came to Live with Us for Three Months*

JUDITH VIORST

Illustrated by Laura Gibson

Free Press
New York   London   Toronto   Sydney

FREE PRESS
A Division of Simon & Schuster, Inc.
1230 Avenue of the Americas
New York, NY 10020

First Free Press hardcover edition October 2007

FREE PRESS and colophon are trademarks of Simon & Schuster, Inc.

For information about special discounts for bulk purchases,
please contact Simon & Schuster Special Sales at
1-800-456-6798 or business@simonandschuster.com

DESIGNED BY ERICH HOBBING

Excerpt from "It's Hard Out Here for a Pimp," written and performed by Three 6 Mafia,
available on Sony Records. Copyright © 2005 by Music Resources, Inc.

Manufactured in the United States of America

1   3   5   7   9   10   8   6   4   2

Library of Congress Cataloging-in-Publication Data
Viorst, Judith.
Alexander and the wonderful, marvelous, excellent, terrific ninety days: an almost completely honest
account of what happened to our family when our youngest son, his wife, their baby, their toddler,
and their fieve-year-old came to live with us for three months / Judith Viorst.
p. cm.
1. Family—Humor. 2. Family life—Humor. I. Title.
HQ536 .V56 2007
306.8709753—dc22   2007016006
ISBN-13: 978-1-4165-5005-1
ISBN-10: 1-4165-5005-4

For Alexander, Marla, Olivia, Isaac, and Toby

Be here now. Be someplace else later. Is that so com-
plicated?

—*Sayings of the Jewish Buddhist*

CONTENTS

CHAPTER ONE

They're Here!

$\mathcal{W}$e are normally a household of two—one husband, one wife—with our children and grandchildren spread near and far in homes of their own. This summer, however, we're sharing our house for ninety (that's ninety) days minimum with our youngest son, Alexander, and his wife, Marla, along with their Olivia (five), Isaac (almost two), and Toby (four months). I am trying to think of this time as a magnificent, once-in-a-lifetime opportunity not only for strengthening family ties and intimately getting to know the grandchildren but for furthering my personal growth while also achieving marital enrichment. I've already resolved to let go of my perhaps excessive commitment to neatness and schedules, and to live in the moment instead of planning ahead, though I'm well aware that many accommodations and even some major transformations may be required. Am I up to the task? Will this really be good for my family, my marriage, and me? And how do I stop my grandchildren from eating on any piece of furniture covered in velvet? I'm about to find out.

I have to admit that Alexander and I had a testy moment *before* they moved in, which they're doing—I ought to point out—

because they're renovating their house, which is, like ours, in Washington, D.C. I had a small suggestion about their renovation plans but I wanted to make my suggestion tactfully. "I know that you and Marla are incredibly competent people," I began, "and quite clear on what you want to do with your house. So feel free to stop me right now if you think I'm being at all intrusive, because I don't want to be the slightest bit intrusive, but I've got a little suggestion that I honestly believe—" Alexander felt free to stop me right now.

"Mom," he said, "those preliminaries of yours? They're SO much more annoying than your advice. So please, just skip them and get to the advice."

I'll have some subsequent testy moments to mention. But right now I'd like to describe our living arrangements.

Ours is a big Victorian house, with a wraparound porch and a balcony overhead. There's a living room, dining room, library, kitchen, and bath on the first floor, and a bedroom, two bathrooms, and two offices (both Milton and I write at home) on the second floor. Our third floor—composed of three bedrooms, one bathroom, one tiny treadmill room, and a central sitting room—is where our three sons grew up and where they sleep when they and their wives and kids come to visit and where the Alexander Five are now living. Over the years we've equipped that third floor with a vast array of child-oriented amenities for the benefit of various visiting grandchildren: toys and games and puzzles, drawing paper and crayons, and large and small stuffed animals and balls, as well as diapers and baby wipes, three different types of car seats, a crib, a stroller, a bouncy seat, a booster seat, a rocking duck, and a potty for those with an interest in toilet training.

What aren't there, what have never been there, and what never will be there are play dough, painting supplies, and containers of glue, on the grounds that no matter how washable such materials claim to be, I don't intend to check out those claims in my house. There are limits to any woman's potential for further personal growth and these, I'm prepared to concede, are some of mine.

Now I've said that the Alexander Five are living on the third floor, but of course they're living in our entire house, though I did have a few secret fantasies about putting up a gate—like a baby gate, except to restrain the whole family. But my mother long ago taught me that when you're going to give you ought to give with both hands and I'm hoping to try, within reason, to follow that rule. So here are the grandchildren, dribbling their drinks in our hallway, playing with mice (the computer kind) in our offices, trying on my jewelry in our bedroom, pushing the TV buttons in our library, and tossing the pillows off our couch in our living room, while their mother and father are trying simultaneously to subdue them and deal with the crises coming over their BlackBerries.

Not that I mean to sound critical of Alexander and Marla's parenting style, which, on a scale from one to ten, is fifteen. They are perfect—well, they are practically perfect—parents, my only reservation being that maybe they do not worry as much as they should. But although our different anxiety levels have made for many an animated discussion, this is, in the larger scheme of things, a quibble. For they meltingly love their kids, delight in their kids, understand their kids, but set limits, teach them manners, discourage whining, lavishing on them kisses and hugs and extravaganzas of praise along with, when needed, a "no" and a "stop that right now." There are certainly times when, sleep-deprived, stressed, and faced with three children screaming simultaneously, Alexander or Marla will say, "If they weren't so adorable, I'd kill them." But remembering, as I well do, my former Desperate Mother days, my "do that one more time and I'll break your kneecaps," I remain full of admiration for the way the two of them balance demanding careers and devoted parenting.

This balancing act, in my humble view, seems harder than it needs to be, for Olivia goes to camp and the others to day care, which means that when they're afflicted with ear infections, rashes, strep, or stomach flu they have to stay home—and there's no one at home to take care of them. Instead, Alexander or Marla leaves work, or they contact an emergency nanny service, or they turn to their backup nannies, Milton and me.

By the way, in case you were wondering, my renovation suggestion to Alexander was adding a room for a nanny or an au pair. I

have many things to say on the subject of why our children don't listen to us when we're offering some brilliant piece of advice, but instead of getting into all that I'm going to introduce you to our family:

Milton and I are the patriarch and matriarch of the Viorsts, having succeeded in staying married for forty-six years, during which time we've acquired three sons (Anthony, Nicholas, and Alexander); three daughters-in-law (Hyla, Marya, and Marla); and a total of seven grandchildren (Miranda and Brandeis, Nathaniel and Benjamin, and Alexander's Olivia, Isaac, and Toby). In addition, our family includes our Taiwanese almost-daughter, Jeannette, and her husband, Steve, the son of my oldest friend, and if all goes well the baby—that would make grandchild number eight—they're eagerly endeavoring to adopt.

We're a fond-of-each-other family and we all get together in Washington three times a year—Thanksgiving, Passover, and a few days in the summer—with all of the out-of-towners, from New York and Denver, squeezing into our house at the same time. This summer, however, the presence of the Alexander Five reduces our sleeping space dramatically, which means that our other kids and their families, instead of coming to Washington simultaneously, are going to have to each make a separate visit. This change in the family tradition has been generating much e-mail on the subject of which of the kids would be coming here when, with the Denver branch—Tony and his crew—deciding on the wide-open spaces of a national park instead of the crowded quarters of D.C. But I have assured everyone that, unless Alexander's contractor misses his deadline (and whoever, I ask you, has heard of such a thing?), we'll return to our joint family visits in November.

Now maybe you think that these joint family visits, three times a year every year, have prepared me for having a family of five in residence. You would be wrong. Did dating prepare me for marriage? Did baby-sitting prepare me for parenthood? Did scrambling an egg prepare me to make a soufflé? So how could a four-day visit, max, after which the whole family departs, prepare me for ninety days, minimum, of this glorious opportunity to enrich my marriage and further my personal growth?

The Alexander Five arrived early in June.

Actually, Alexander moved into our house a few days before the rest of the family because Marla had taken the children to visit her parents and because renovations were dustily under way. He arrived with hangers and suitcases full of summer wardrobes for everyone, including Olivia's pink-sequined flip-flops and Supergirl shirt. He arrived with cartons of toys and books, and hair and beauty products, and kids' DVDs. He arrived with a jogger, a baby swing, one wagon, two cars, and four bicycles, all of them his. He even arrived with his own special coffee and pot, which spurred my husband to loudly complain, "What—the coffee I make in this house isn't good enough?"

He arrived with possessions sufficient to fill every inch of the third floor, plus some nooks and crannies of the rooms below. He arrived with the contents of their freezer and fridge. Some fifteen sweaty trips later he had transferred whatever was needed from their house to ours, and had settled into the bedroom of his boyhood.

And soon after that, I reverted to the mommy of his boyhood, which quickly led to another testy moment.

For Alexander would go off to work and then to a baseball game, a movie, a dinner, not mentioning his plans or when he'd be back. The first night this happened, watching the late evening hours tick-tocking by, I worked myself into a panic attack. The next night this happened, I called him on his cell phone, just to make sure that he was alive and well.

Alexander took the position that he was thirty-nine years old, and didn't need to routinely check in with his mother. I took the position that when adults were living together in a household—no matter which of them was the parent of whom—they were obliged, out of courtesy, out of simple human decency, to notify each other of their whereabouts. "Otherwise, we'll never know," I told him, "when to call the hospitals and the police."

How can you argue with that? Alexander did.

"This arrangement isn't going to work," he informed me, "if I have to hear how you're worried all the time. I can't be thinking I need to call my mommy." My husband, who doesn't worry because he has put me in charge of worrying, treacherously agreed with Alexander.

Well, maybe this is how women are different from men. For the fact is, we mothers don't stop being mothers because our children are grown. We remain in a state I have elsewhere called Permanent Parenthood. Our concern and our need to protect our kids become especially strong when, whatever their age, they're living under our roof, and we surely would worry less if they would be kind enough to inform us where they are going and when they plan to be back (just as long as they're back when they say they will be). Indeed, when I later conducted a poll of some mothers of middle-aged children, ten out of ten of those women supported my view, but I didn't need to pursue this point with my own middle-aged baby boy because Marla and the children would soon be arriving. With Marla in the house, I happily reassured myself, this thorny issue would be rendered moot. For although Alexander might feel that he doesn't have to check in with his mother, I suspect he'll be checking in plenty with his wife.

And then she arrived, my beautiful golden-haired daughter-in-law, with her adorable, weary, weeping, food-stained brood, surging into the house with what looked to be two dozen more pieces of equipment. I felt delighted to see them and eager to help them settle in, but I also felt, a bit, as if they were General Sherman's troops marching through my Civil War Atlanta. Listening to my tale of family love and occupation, my friend Hanna later offered a helpful perspective. "Be grateful," she said as she poured me a generous glass of Chardonnay. "Just be grateful they don't own a dog."

This same friend also reminded me that her recent, unhappy kitchen renovation was supposed to take two months and took thirteen, due to the nonappearance for weeks on end of her outrageously feckless contractor. A deeply nonviolent person, she nonetheless had this to say after more than a year of eating out in restaurants: "If Osama bin Laden and my contractor were walking down the street and I had a gun in my purse and that gun had two bullets, I would use up both those bullets on my contractor to make absolutely sure he was dead."

She said that the point of her story was not to reveal the heart of darkness lurking in all of us or even to show she was weak on the War Against Terrorism, but simply to prepare me for the not-too-remote possibility that we all might still be together come next January.

I decided to put off preparing for that possibility.

I have, however, drawn up a list of some of my wishes and needs—okay, call them house rules— that I hope will be indulged in the weeks ahead,  although I have no intention of actually showing this list to Marla or Alexander. Instead I plan, with my trademark nonchalance, to slip these items into our conversations, dropping them in so casually that they'll never even notice that I have suggested them. My only problem with this plan, as Milton has pointed out, is I've never been known for my trademark nonchalance.

Here are some of the items on my list:

1. Of all of the places that chocolate shouldn't be eaten, the number-one place is the wine-velvet chair in the library. Please note, this applies to everyone, not just to children.
2. You shouldn't set drinking glasses on wood surfaces, like a table or the floor. If you do, you'll leave permanent circles on those surfaces. For those who believe this is not necessarily true I have one thing to say: Don't do it anyway.
3. No child should ever enter my home office unless he or she is accompanied by an adult. The keys of my com-

puter are not meant for banging on. The backs of my manuscript pages are not meant for coloring on. My files are not meant to be shaken out of their beige manila folders in order to turn the folders into tents. I'm pointing the finger at no one. They know who they are.

4. I need the remote controls to be exactly where I put them. And nowhere else. I don't want the children to touch them. I don't want kids or adults to relocate them. I don't want, when I want them, to have to look for them. I also don't want to be told that, if they get lost, I can always replace them and—no problem—learn how to use the (to me invariably incomprehensible) replacements, especially when it comes to figuring out how to track down reruns of *The Sopranos*. And if someone has an opinion on how it's a waste of my time to watch reruns of *The Sopranos,* please don't tell me about it.

5. My beautiful flowered dinner dishes must be washed by hand although they are guaranteed to be "dishwasher safe." "Dishwasher safe" may be good enough for the other adults in this household but it simply isn't good enough for me, for even the safest dishwasher dishes will sometimes chip and crack, and I hate chips and cracks. To those who would suggest that I'm neurotic about my beautiful flowered dishes, I hereby concede that—yes, okay—I'm neurotic. Now let's just wash the goddamn dishes by hand.

6. There is ice cream, diet and regular, on the top shelf of my freezer. The second and third shelves hold chicken parts and meats. The fourth shelf is for hors d'oeuvres and packs of smoked salmon and frozen soups and frozen vegetables. The fifth shelf holds bread, plus cake and other sweets. This is the way I like it. This is the way I want it. Does anybody have a problem with that?

7. Since this subject has often come up, I would like to make myself perfectly clear about how to deal with my lack of certain skills: Last year, when I bought my cell phone, Alexander tried to instruct me in making and answering calls (which I finally mastered) and retrieving my telephone messages (which I could not). He solved the problem, to my satisfaction and his enormous disgust, by recording the following inhospitable words: "Judith Viorst does not receive any messages. Keep on trying until she answers the phone." I'm mentioning this because, with my children living right here in my house, my absence of electronic and other such skills might (a) become more obvious and irritating to them and (b) tempt them to teach me things I do not wish to know: Like how to take a photograph with my cell phone. Or how to listen to music on my computer. Or what to do with a TiVo or an iPod.

   I need it to be understood that, unless I'm asking how to do it, I don't want to do it.

8. Since this subject has also often come up, I would like

to make myself clear about how to deal with what's viewed as my overprotectiveness. For when it comes to matters having to do with the physical safety of my grandchildren, there is—in my view—no such thing as overprotectiveness.

For instance, before they all moved in, I carefully checked out the house for sources of possible injury or worse and, after a careful survey of upstairs and downstairs, inside and out, I found that the possibilities were endless: Choking on the cashew nuts sitting in a bowl on our living-room coffee table. Impaling themselves on one of the exceedingly sharp corners of that coffee table. Gouging out an eye with a fireplace poker. Electrocuting themselves by sticking their finger into the toaster to pull out the toast. Crushing a toe or a foot by knocking over the marble sculpture on our hutch table. Poisoning themselves by dragging my blue chair from my bedroom into the bathroom and climbing on that chair to reach the medicine chest and figuring out—because they're exceptionally brilliant—how to pry the safety cap off of one of our fatal bottles of pills. There is also the possibility of running out the front door and into our street, which looks like a country lane but in fact is not, for maniacal driving-way-too-fast drivers, taking a wrong turn, can threaten the very lives of little children. There is, in

addition, falling—falling out of, falling off of, and falling down from, about which I am especially obsessed. Let me explain:

When my sons were little boys they shared a hamster who lived in a cage on the third floor. One night the hamster escaped from his cage, slipped between the railings of our stairway, and plunged straight down to the hall of our first floor. Miraculously he survived and managed to live for a few more years but I always believed that he suffered from serious brain damage, though people keep pointing out to me that it's really hard to tell if a hamster has brain damage. In any case, this accident has left me with the fear that a child will fall from the third to the first floor, though people keep pointing out to me that the three-inch space between railings is enough for a hamster but not for a child to squeeze through. I fault these people for lacking an appropriate degree of overprotectiveness.

And so, while my grandchildren live here, they will live in a childproofed house, in which I intend to be shamelessly overprotective. Issuing frequent warnings. Assuming that if they can, they will do themselves harm. Treating the sounds of silence not as children playing quietly together but as children engaged in something that is likely to lead to a trip to the ER. I don't care that this hypervigilance will seriously curtail my summer reading. I don't care that it will also curtail my sleep. All that I am asking from the other adults in this house is for no one to say, "Don't worry so much. Relax."

I honestly don't think that is too much to ask.

I'm aware that I am sounding a lot less relaxed and a lot less flexible than I aspire to be by the end of the summer. But let's see what happens as the weeks progress. Milton and I have vowed to protect our sweet connection with Alexander's family, in spite of the noise, lack of privacy, and mess. Indeed, I'm expecting us all to transcend the conflicts bound to arise in the course of our intense and intimate living together. I'm also still expecting, if I can calm down about the velvet, to even achieve a little personal growth.

CHAPTER TWO

Feeding Frenzy

*O*n weekdays Marla and Alexander arise at the dawn's early light, either rousing or being roused by their children, and instantly swing into their dress-them, feed-them, let's-get-out-of-here-fast morning mode. When I emerge from my bedroom at 7:15 or 7:30 (Milton will follow fifteen or so minutes later), Olivia, fully dressed and sitting crossed-legged on the floor outside my door, announces in reverential tones more suitable to "Elvis is leaving the building" that "JuJu"—that's my grandmother name—"is up."

Down in the kitchen I open my arms to a soft warm bundle of Toby, who guzzles his bottle of formula solemnly, tightly gripping my pinky and gazing deeply into my eyes as if I alone hold the secret of his happiness. Isaac, puffing his cheeks out and then punching them with his fists to make a satisfying pop-pop-pop-pop sound, is greeting me with the trick I recently taught him. And although I wish he would think of me as his storybook-reading rather than cheek-punching JuJu, I am feeling warmly welcomed by my temporarily irresistible grandchildren.

The operative word, of course, is "temporarily."

Marla and Alexander, on their feet and on the move, are swilling down bites of bagel and cups of coffee while also matching small shoes to small feet, ponytailing a tangle of long yellow hair, preparing Olivia's lunch and Isaac's snack and a couple of Toby's backup bottles, stuffing the food and some changes of clothes and various other necessities into backpacks, and persuading two, sometimes three, of the kids simultaneously that they still love the breakfast they loved ten seconds ago. But Isaac is dumping his Cheerios on the floor. And Toby is letting us know, via screams, that happiness can no longer be found in a bottle. And Olivia is defending her right to eat a bowl of berries that consists of three measly berries and eight spoons of sugar.

"Hey, girlfriend," Alexander says to Olivia. "The idea is berries with sugar, not sugar with berries."

Olivia isn't accepting these proportions. Nor is Isaac accepting a box of Frosted Flakes as an alternative to his rejected Cheerios. Nor is Toby accepting a pacifier as a replacement for his once-beloved, now apparently hated bottle. There is, at the moment, much crying in the kitchen.

Marla and Alexander, scolding, cajoling, comforting, chastising, pleading, insisting, and sometimes threatening dire punishment, focus on getting their family ready to leave. Miraculously they are able to make this happen. And they're on their way to work, driving downtown in two separate cars with the children strapped into three different versions of car seats, Marla and Olivia going off in one direction, Alexander and the two boys in another. Milton, who has made coffee—*his* special coffee—for himself and me, brings our breakfast and newspapers out on the porch. And unless a grandchild is ill and we have volunteered to be the default nan-

nies, the day—give or take a few toys and games and Cheerios and crayons and some sandals and Junior Suffragist shirts to pick up—is all ours.

Milton and I are exhausted just from watching our son and daughter-in-law negotiate these high-octane early mornings, sometimes with colds or stomach flu and always on impossibly little sleep. The spillage, both liquid and solid, is often torrential. The din and the demands go on nonstop. But Marla has said of the parent-career-marriage juggling act they engage in that she feels that they are much luckier than most. "Alex and I share the child care fifty-fifty," she explains. "And my bosses couldn't be more understanding. Plus our children are healthy, our day care is great, and you and Milton are living right here in town. I know plenty of working moms who have none of these."

In addition, Marla's parents—both of them younger, thinner, and stronger, not to mention more glamorous, than we are—can be called on from time to time to fly from their Michigan home to Washington, D.C., where they'll free their daughter and son-in-law to go away for a weekend while they baby-sit.

And yet, with all this support, Marla adds, "I still would have to say that we're always living on the brink of chaos. Even with all of the pieces in place, even with everybody being helpful, things can sometimes start falling apart because families and children can be so unpredictable."

With a gift for contingency planning that puts FEMA and Homeland Security to shame, Alexander and Marla are unlikely ever to let things fall apart.

Their just-in-case scenarios, their months-in-advance advance planning, their lists of people to call when the people they're counting on to show up fail to show up, appear to cover every possibility. But by the time they've finished doing their best by their three children and their careers, there isn't too much left over for personal pleasures. Having it all, says Marla, is not an option.

"Someday I'll play the piano again and work out every day, plant a vegetable garden, do regular volunteer work, spend more time with my husband, and entertain like Martha Stewart instead of serving salsa, chips, and beer. But right now?" she unapologetically tells me. "Right now there's no Martha Stewart in my life."

Nor, right now, is there much Martha Stewart in mine.

Indeed, when our friends come by for a drink before we go out to a restaurant together, we drink—if it's not too blazing hot—on our porch. For although the Alexander Five have colonized that porch with a jogger, a buggy, a couple of strollers, some balls, a helmet and bike, and four extremely large and ugly bright green plastic boxes from Peapod's home-delivered groceries service, it still looks better out there than it does inside. Inside isn't looking too good not only because of the kids' stuff scattered all over the floors and not only because the tops of our front-hall radiator covers now display two different sizes of diapers (some unused, some used) and two different strengths of sunscreen (for infants, for children) and pacifiers in two distinctive styles. It also isn't looking too good because all our household grace notes—the vases of flow-

ers, the painted Russian boxes, the coffee-table art books, the charming knickknacks, the glass bowls filled with candy or potpourri—have been removed, to save them from being damaged or lost forever, from every (at least I hope every) child-reachable surface. And since child-reachable surfaces include what Isaac is able to reach when he enterprisingly pushes a chair to the object of his affections and then climbs up on it, our first floor is a sorry and most un-Martha combination of stark, strewn, and stinky.

Our dining habits have also taken a dive since the arrival of the Alexander Five.

For when there were just the two of us, Milton and I habitually sat down to a quiet dinner at 6:45, the perfect compromise between his wish to have dinner at 8 and my preference for dinner at 5:30. Though we constantly watch our weight, and though we often eat our dinner in the kitchen, we still like dining graciously and well, which involved—in the good old days—the use of cloth napkins and our beautiful flowered plates, and a glass or maybe two of a quite decent wine, and a main course that might be a veal *piccata,* a poppy-seed-crusted tuna, or chicken breasts in a mustard-ginger sauce.

Often, while we were eating, there would be mellow music playing in the background—the Modern Jazz Quartet or Simon and Garfunkel. We'd discuss everything from the state of the world to the veal. Dinner was, in our postchildren years, a highly civilized meal. And someday it will be that way again.

Someday, when there are just two instead of seven of us, it will be that way again.

At the moment, however, we're still in search of the answers to several questions. Like: When and where will who be eating what? And, can't the children use napkins instead of sleeves? And, shouldn't someone sometimes try a vegetable? And, couldn't Olivia learn, when she sees a grown-up eating something that she believes to be utterly revolting, to stop saying "yuck" and making vomit noises? Actually, I've invented a little rhyme to recite to Olivia whenever she begins her "yuck" routine. It goes:

Don't be rude
About other people's food.

And since she now recites the poem (after she does the "yuck" and the vomiting noises), I think that we're beginning to make some progress.

We hope to make some progress on other fronts. For instance, Milton and I and Alexander and Marla agree that we won't aspire to togetherness at mealtimes. We agree that Milton and I will plan to eat at more or less our usual time and the rest of the gang will do dinner catch-as-catch-can. Here, on a typical Wednesday, is how this plays out:

I've set the kitchen table for two, with four other help-yourself settings stacked on the counter, and I'm making food enough for us all to eat—Milton and I in ten minutes, the others whenever. Marla has arrived, having picked up Olivia on her way home from her office. Alexander has arrived, having picked up Isaac and Toby on his way home. Marla is heating a baby bottle, and Milton is cooking the older children pasta, and Alexander is trying to comfort a famished and wailing Toby, and Isaac is playing peek-a-boo under the table, and Olivia is drawing on her special Olivia pad on top of the table, and I've just spilled gravy on the kitchen floor, and Olivia now has slipped on the gravied floor, and we're mopping her off and serving her her pasta, and Isaac is saying "no, no, no" to his pasta, and our background music is Isaac's "no"s and Toby's diminishing sobs and Olivia merrily singing to the somewhat frazzled adults, "If you're happy and you know it, clap your hands."

Wine helps. Filling Toby's belly with formula helps. Using the plain, unflowered dishes helps, because then I'm not compelled to say, "You've got to stop banging that flowered dish with your sippy cup." Accepting less than elegant manners helps. Getting accustomed to kids bobbing up and down from the table between bites of pasta helps. And so does the absence of jazz and "hello, darkness, my old friend," for we can't handle any more music while Olivia is singing her never-ending verses of "If you're happy . . ."

Milton and I are no longer clapping our hands.

Throughout this meal, let me note, Alexander and Marla are responsibly telling their children to remember their pleases and thank yous, and use their napkins and try not to slurp, and that pasta is for eating not for wearing. They also are scolding Olivia for giving Isaac a poke when he tries to steal her zigzag straw from her glass. They also are offering Isaac some alluring replacements for that zigzag straw but his position, unarticulated but totally,

screamingly clear is, "Accept no substitutes." They also are holding, walking, bouncing, feeding, talking to Toby, who, although normally cheerful, is now inconsolable. And they also are, at dessert time, sternly limiting their children's supply of sweets, though Olivia—whose middle name surely should have been Let's Make a Deal—is a tough negotiator.

"One mini Dove Bar for you, little O," says her mother.

"Four," Olivia brazenly replies.

"Four—are you crazy? One," her mother tells her.

"JuJu always lets me have three," she lies.

"Never," I say indignantly, though I *sometimes* let her have three, but not when her mother or father is anyplace near.

Olivia silently raises her hand, smiles her killer smile, and waggles two slender fingers in the air, soon after which she is eating TWO mini Dove Bars.

And Isaac, outraged, starts yelling, "Mine! Mine! Mine!"

Soon after which *he* is eating two mini Dove Bars.

I've always said that, when raising kids, you must establish and stand by certain principles. I never said you should stand by them all the time. And so, as far as I'm concerned, let them each have *three* mini Dove Bars, so long as they stay in the kitchen, where nothing is velvet.

I feel a need to explain my concerns about velvet.

During the years that Milton and I were raising three boisterous boys, we decorated our house appropriately, choosing fabrics and furniture better known for their endurance than for their charm. We wanted our sons and their friends to feel welcome and comfortable in our home, which meant that fragile furnishings would not do, and which especially meant that the sofas and chairs I was longing to upholster in elegant velvets would be covered in sturdier fabrics, like corduroy.

I really loved velvet. I didn't much love corduroy.

But I bided my time and eventually my children grew up and got places of their own, freeing me for a less defensive décor. And over the next several years the stain-resistant corduroys gave way to rooms full of velvet, delicate velvets, glorious velvets, more velvet (some have suggested) than anyone needs. I had bided my time and my sons were grown and now it was safe to have sofas and chairs of velvet. Except I had failed to factor in the grandchildren.

Who, by the time I had fully finished velveting the house, began to arrive.

Now I don't think I have to say that I love my grandchildren more, far more, than I love velvet. But why must I choose?

And so, whenever they visit, I attend lovingly to their needs while standing between drooling babies and golden velvet, between runny-nosed toddlers and deep rich burgundy velvet, between pre-scholars clutching melting M&M's in both their hands and a subtly striped (mostly fawn and celery) velvet, between kids oozing catsup and mustard and peanut butter and cherry pie and a lushly patterned brown-bronze-mocha velvet.

I have waged, until the moving in of the Alexander Five, tough but successful battles against the forces that would violate my velvets. But now that I'm facing attacks that are both daily and sustained from my three enchanting but often smeary grandchildren, I am, for the first time, fearful for their survival . . . . The survival, that is, of my velvets—not of my grandchildren.

In addition to breakfasts and dinners each day, and lunches on the weekends, there's a great deal of in-between eating known as the "snack," which is why my glass-windowed kitchen cabinets (once so neatly arranged that sometimes I would actually stand there admiring them) are now a jammed-in-all-together helter-skelter mess of animal crackers, fishy crackers, mini-muffins, tiny cartons of applesauce, miniature boxes of Gatorade, miniature boxes of cereal, and (take your choice) either Scooby-Doo or Dora the Explorer fruit-flavored snacks.

Isaac, who has the plump rounded beauty of a Renaissance cherub, can also be found admiring my cabinets, his beseeching brown eyes and his piteous cries as he gazes at the goodies behind

the glass conveying a state of criminal starvation. Trying to carry his oh-too-solid flesh past the cabinets and onto a kitchen chair poses a challenge to the lower back. And trying to sell him on carrots when he's yearning for Scooby-Doos poses a challenge similar to selling George W. Bush on tax increases.

Snacks are much preferred to meals and are eaten far more frequently and copiously—before and after breakfast, lunch, and dinner. And, unlike meals, which in theory are eaten only in the kitchen, snacks are carried to every room of the house. My supermarket sojourns, which, despite those boxes of home-delivered groceries, take place about four out of seven days a week, can barely keep pace with this voracious consumption. Nor can my DustBuster suck up the smushed and spilled and stomped and crumbled food debris as fast as Isaac and his big sister create it. The tidiest of the three children is Toby, whose repertoire is limited to the bottle, though Milton and I tend to call it the "fucking bottle," because it is merely a shell into which—each time and for us with great difficulty—you insert a disposable condom-like plastic sheath. And should you forget to insert the sheath (as both Milton and I will sometimes forget to do) and pour the warmed formula into this shell of a bottle, you'll soon be mopping formula off the floor.

Our ineptitude with the bottle extends to our failure to master the locks of Toby's bouncy seat, safety locks designed, we've been assured, to protect a baby from falling out of his seat and not for the specific purpose of torturing his hopelessly klutzy grandparents. So Toby is locked in his bouncy seat, screaming for his bottle. And Milton and I have finally prepared his bottle. And now we need to unlock the locks and lift Toby into our arms and feed him his bottle. The unlocking part of this plan isn't going too well.

"Press down here, and pull there," I say to Milton.

"I'm pressing. I'm pulling. It isn't working," he says.

"I think we need to release that center part first," I say to Milton.

"I already tried. It won't release," he says.

"Or maybe we could just slide his little arms out from under the harness," I say to Milton.

"Get out of my light and stop talking," Milton says.

Eventually, thanks to a not-very-gracious team effort, Milton and I spring Toby from his bouncy seat. He no longer has any interest in his bottle.

Cleaning up the kitchen at the end of a three-meal, five-or-six-snack day, Milton, munching his grandchildren's leftovers as he does the dishes, seems to have discovered his inner child. "This mac 'n' cheese is pretty good," he tells me. Or, popping some soggy frozen pizza into the toaster oven and then devouring it, he pronounces it to be "not bad at all." He turns rather haughty, however, when I offer him some fruit-flavored Scooby-Doos. "Certainly not," he says. "I have my standards."

But our standards, as I have made clear, are not what they used to be. With the velvet imperiled, the flowered dishes unused, the state of our house not something you'd want friends to see, the kitchen shelves in tumult, the shelves of our freezer and fridge beyond description, the sound of silence replaced by the sound of crying, and gracious dining no more than a distant memory, the phrase I keep holding on to is, "This too shall pass."

Then Isaac flings himself at me and gives my knees a fiercely

passionate hug. And Toby sleeps in my arms with sighs of content-
ment. And Olivia puts her small hand in mine and says, "Let's take
a shower and dress up stylish." And Alexander and Marla share a
quiet drink with us at the end of an evening. And maybe I really
don't want this to pass too soon.

CHAPTER THREE

The Resident Grandchildren

*O*livia never walks down the stairs of our house. Actually, she rarely even runs down them. Her preferred travel mode is the jump: Three steps from the bottom. Four steps from the bottom. Five steps from the . . .

"Stop that, Olivia. Stop that right now," shouts her father. "One of these days you're really going to hurt yourself."

Alexander pretends that he can't possibly imagine where his daughter acquired such risk-embracing behavior. All of us know, however, that the gene was passed directly to her from him. As a person who, at Olivia's age, climbed onto the wing of the plane ride at the amusement park because riding on the inside was just too boring, Alexander is reaping what he has sowed. Once upon a time he used to call me—fondly, I tell myself—his paranoid and overprotective mother. Now, and I must admit I take some pleasure in recording this, he is me.

(Well, *almost* me. I still could give him a few instructions in worrying.)

The past is also repeating itself in other, less potentially perilous ways. For instance:

O and I are sitting on the wall-to-wall carpeted floor of my home office, where I'm teaching her the art of building card houses. "Find the balance," I urge her as her tented structures wobble and collapse. She grows increasingly frustrated and I try to help by offering her a mantra: "Cats meow, dogs bark, pigs oink, and card houses fall down," I briskly say to her. The mantra seems to work. We keep on building.

My husband, watching us building, sneezes loudly, sneezes again, then sneezes once more. Our house is going up. Uh-oh, it's down. "Cats meow," says Olivia. "Dogs bark. Pigs oink. Card houses fall down. And papas sneeze—very very loudly."

We start all over. Persistence finally pays off. We construct a house using every card in the deck. Alexander, standing at the doorway of my office, is grinning broadly.

"I sat on this floor and I did the same thing when I was a little boy," he tells Olivia. "I sat right here and my mom taught *me* to build card houses."

With Olivia in my life on a daily basis, there are many other things I am able to teach her. Like checkers and a variety of board games. Like word games: What's the opposite of "happy"? Can you give me three words that rhyme with "bite"? And like a bouncing-ball alphabet game from my childhood that begins—pick your own nouns: "'A' my name is Anna and my husband's name is Albert and we come from Alabama and we bring back apples. 'B' my name is Betsy and . . ." straight through to "Zelda, Zero, Zimbabwe, and zebras." Try it; you'll like it.

We also draw pictures, sitting side by side at the kitchen table, and do jigsaw puzzles, at which she's much better than I. "JuJu," she often says, quite patronizingly, to me, "if you'd practiced puzzles instead of reading so much when you were little, you wouldn't be so terrible at them now." But after completing her sixty-piece puzzle in truly record time, she always condescends to help me with mine.

"I'm good at doing puzzles," she says. "I'm good at writing books," I reply defensively. "Different people have different things they're good at." And later, when I'm moaning about how incredibly long it's taking me to fit just four of these stupid pieces together, Olivia gives me a pat on my hand and reminds me, "Different people have different things they're good at."

As the mother of three sons who rarely if ever patted my hand and who dressed and smelled like street people till the day that they discovered the opposite sex, I've found it a revelation to have two granddaughters, especially since both of them (despite O's risky habits) are deliciously, unequivocally girly-girls. My firstborn— hazel-eyed, movie-star-gorgeous Miranda—lives far away, in Denver, Colorado, which means that even with visits back and forth on agonizing United Airlines we see each other just five or six times a year. (Though now that she has acquired her own e-mail address, we may begin to be in more frequent contact.)

Because they're less regularly in our lives, we don't know our Denver grandchildren or our New York ones as day-to-day intimately as the ones from D.C. We're aware that Brandeis, aka Bryce, is at seven an adept and passionate athlete, and almost impossible to beat at checkers. We're aware that Nathaniel, age four, is a gutsy kid who, even when scared, will physically challenge himself, and who loves riding scooters and making up games with his friends, and whose powers of persuasion can get his parents to do what he wants, even if they've already said no three times. We're aware that Benjamin, just turned two, can count to fifty and speak in perfect sentences and may, in our humble opinion, be a genius. And we're also aware that Miranda (along with being a fine artist, an avid reader, and wonderfully sweet with all of the younger kids) is a major Fashion Person, with—at the age of only eleven—the best, most inventive taste in the whole family.

In a talk with Miranda on the subject of our shared pleasure in clothes, I once said that I thought it was quite okay to be a Fashion Person as long as that wasn't the only thing we were, as long as we cared about clothes within the context of larger matters that we cared about. I told her that we were allowed to be concerned about purses *and* peace, and I plan to discuss this with O when she's a bit older. But right now we simply revel in dressing up after taking a leisurely shower together—since she moved in I rarely shower alone—while checking out each other's choices in dresses and skirts, in pants, sweaters, shoes, and jewelry. We also do makeup together, playing with powder and lipstick and blush—"Don't want to look like a clown," she repeats after me. And if she or I, in her judgment, has managed to put ourselves together especially well, she'll confer upon us her ultimate accolade: "Stylish!"

Olivia—who has never displayed any problems with low self-esteem—has made it clear that she views herself as not only a lot more stylish but also much better-looking than her grandma. She decides to solicit her grandfather's concurrence.

> Olivia: "So Papa, who is prettier—JuJu or me?"
> Milton: "I wouldn't answer that for a million dollars."
> Olivia: "Please Papa, say it—which of us is prettier?"
> Milton: "I already told you—I won't answer that question."
> Olivia: "Please Papa, please Papa, please, please, please. I need you to answer the question just this once. Which of us is prettier—JuJu or me?"

This dialogue goes on for a while. Milton is hanging tough. But Olivia is utterly relentless. And after a ferocious barrage of "I need you"s and "just this once"s and "please, Papa, please"s, Milton, fool that he is, finally capitulates. "Well, I guess I'd have to say JuJu, because she's my wife."

Olivia's face is a study in shocked disbelief. "JuJu?" she squeals. "JuJu you picked? How could you do that?"

Milton explains once again. "Because JuJu's my wife."

"Okay, okay, okay," says an outraged O, "JuJu's your wife. But I"—and here she speaks in the stentorian tones of God addressing Moses—"I am your *granddaughter*."

On and off for the next twelve hours Olivia complains about Milton's response, commanding and begging him to reconsider and calling upon her mother and father and even upon me to declare him some version of mentally incompetent. I see a family resemblance here: When my mother entered a beauty contest in high school, she came in second and promptly demanded a recount. As a result, the caption under her high-school yearbook read, "Ruth Ehrenkranz, most conceited girl in the class." This is another discussion that I'll be having with Olivia when she is older.

One weekend in early July the New York contingent—Marya, Nick, Nathaniel, and Benjamin—bravely drove down to D.C. for their summer visit, increasing to eleven the number of relatives stuffed into our bulging house. There are rituals to be followed whenever our sons and their families return to the old homestead: Making room in our driveway for their automobiles. Selecting suitable grown-up and kid DVDs. Meeting their eating requirements—Atkins for this one, vegetarian for that one, whole milk, two percent, one percent, fat-free. And checking out the family photos hanging on the walls of our second-floor hall to make sure that there is equal representation. Aren't our sons too old to be counting up photographs and complaining, "There's two more pictures of Tony than of me?" It seems they are not.

While Isaac and Benjamin warily eyed each other, O and Nathaniel bonded instantly, shouting and laughing and racing each other up and down the stairs, shining flashlights into each other's faces, swimming together, bathing together, showering together, and—with some assistance from Isaac and Benjamin—together transforming my still somewhat orderly office into a wall-to-wall full-service playroom. "What's all that stuff?" they asked about the hectic collection of drawings, photos, and messages I've tacked to the bulletin board behind my desk. I skipped past "For peace of mind, resign as general manager of the universe," and read them another favorite, a picture postcard from a far-off friend: "The last time I saw you, besides that memorable fall day when we all marched on the Justice Department and shouted, 'Stop the war!' to whoever was listening, was in the Giant on Wisconsin Avenue. You were pulling two loaded grocery carts and three boys."

The children of two of these now-grown-up boys, having finally finished working over my office, moved on to Milton's, where they swarmed all over the room and persuaded their papa to quit the computer and come play. Not that it was so hard to persuade him to play. For Milton, having grown up as an only child, had always longed for brothers and sisters. His sons, in a sense, had helped to meet that need, providing him later in life with built-in buddies to horse around with, go canoeing with, camp with, ski with, play Sunday-morning softball with, and discuss in minute-by-minute detail every triumph and every tragedy of the Redskins with. As the grandchildren started arriving, Milton looked forward to grooming them for similar roles, delighted he had so many of them to groom. Indeed, on the grounds of the more grandchildren the merrier, he offered—after our sons and their wives declared themselves holding the line at two kids apiece—a bonus payment for a seventh grandchild. We learned of the impending addition of Toby to our clan when Marla and Alexander came over to see us one day, announcing that they were there for the bonus payment. Milton, proud as could be of the success of his plan to increase the Viorst population, was thrilled to pay up.

And now he was thrilled to be hanging out with four of his seven grandchildren—Isaac and Benjamin, Nathaniel and O. Lying down on his rug with his knees drawn up and his hands holding on to a giggling Nathaniel, whose belly was shakily balanced on Milton's knees, and assuring the other kids that yes, if they'd please wait a minute—please!—they'd each get a turn, my husband gave me a look that said as plainly as any words: "This is exactly what it's all about."

I agreed. Which didn't mean that either of us was anything less than eager for their bedtime.

Because the bodies exceeded the beds, we spread sleeping bags on the third floor, embedding each body in its proper location. But during the course of the night many ups and downs, ins and outs, and rearrangements occurred. Alexander, for instance, discovered that sometime after midnight Isaac and O had both joined Marla in bed while he, Alexander, was now dispossessed and lying on the floor, zipped cozily into a red-checked, fuzzy-pawed, absolutely adorable puppy-dog sleeping bag.

A good time, though little sleep, was had by all.

Well, except for poor Nathaniel, who, the next day, skipped breakfast and wound up in the ER, where he and his dependably calm and patient mother, Marya, and I spent a good three hours making sure that his stomach pains were nothing serious. Sitting in the waiting room, I remembered earlier times, too many to count, when Nathaniel's dad and his uncles were rushed to the hospital, rushed there for broken wrists, smashed noses, knocked-out teeth, heavy bleeding, falls on the head, and—at one devilish brother's suggestion to his younger brother—the drinking of turpentine.

I have many tender memories of my long-ago days as the mother of small boys. Our visits to the emergency rooms of Washington, D.C., are not among them.

To celebrate Nathaniel's escape from appendicitis and other major ills, and also to reward him for courageously enduring pokes, prods, and needles, we drove straight from the hospital to the toy store. There we bought him a special gift and some lesser gifts for all of the other children, returning him home with a smile on his face and ready for the wild rumpus to resume.

Later that day Nathaniel, who has been working on his manners, was asked by his parents to demonstrate his new mannerliness.

Nick: "What do you say when you get a present you like?"

Nathaniel: "Thank you."

Marya: "And what do you say when you get a present you don't like?"

Nathaniel: "Thank you."

Nick: "And what do you say when you get a present you really, really hate?"

Nathaniel: "Thank you."

Marya: "And later you can come and discuss it with me."

A round of cheers and applause was offered by all.

Before the visit was over I imprinted the older grandchildren with glittery, wash-offable tattoos, the sticking on of which has lately become another Viorst family ritual. These silver tattoos, in the shape of diamonds or spirals or hearts or stars, are actually, if you must know, *my* tattoos, which I sometimes wear on my upper right arm as a way of informing the world that I'M STILL HERE. But my grandchildren, as they've grown older, have come to admire them and to covet them, reminding me that it's not nice not to share. And so on Sunday morning O and Nathaniel arrived in my bedroom, made their selection, lifted an arm in the air, and waited while their grandma peeled off the paper, pressed down the picture, and tattooed them.

When the New Yorkers departed I thought of the folk tale of the peasant who bitterly complained that his hut was too small. He was told to bring in his chickens, his goat, and his pig. He lived with these animals for a while, then put them back outside, and suddenly found that his hut was plenty big. In this same spirit I found, when Marya, Nick, Nathaniel, and Benjamin went home (and we love them, we miss them, we want them back, we do!) that our house, reduced to merely seven inhabitants, had all of a sudden become palatial.

I intend, when O is older and complains about this or that, to discuss the concept of "as compared to what?"

* * *

There are many discussions I'm planning to have with Olivia and her brothers and her cousins. There are many messages that I wish to impart. There are also skills and planets and poems I'm intending to introduce them to. And there are, as well, excursions and adventures I'm hoping that we can engage in together, shared pleasures I hope that in later life they'll recall.

Indeed, I think a great deal—maybe more than I ought to—of how I would like my grandchildren to remember me. But if it's considered legitimate for presidents to care about their legacies, why can't a grandma?

I'm working on my legacies right now.

And right now my legacy with cherubic Isaac, our resident almost-two-year-old, is lessons in pillow fights and Follow the Leader, a game that includes the puffing of cheeks as well as the tapping of heads, the rubbing of bellies, the pinching of noses and chins, the waggling of ears, the sticking out of tongues, and the twirling around and around and around till the game finally ends in falling down or giggles. He's sensational at giggles and he shrieks with delight as he chugs around the house, looking for food, for trouble, and for fun. And a recent report from day care, after a day during which he was feeling none too well, nonetheless said that "Isaac tries hard to be happy." Still my heart aches a bit for sweet Isaac because Toby's birth was only seventeen months after his, and because he wants more from his mommy than his mommy, or daddy, or any of us can offer him. Indeed, the other morning, when everybody's attention seemed to be focused on Toby, Isaac silently watched from the sidelines and then announced, just in case we hadn't noticed, "*Isaac* a baby."

I'd like, as part of my Isaac legacy, to help him have his chance to still be a baby.

Toby, at the moment, is the easiest of the three children, though sleep doesn't seem to be part of his CV, asking no more of life than to be fed, changed, cuddled, tickled, bounced, and talked to, and inviting us to respond in kind to his exuberant production of chortles and coos. Unaware, as yet, of competitive feelings toward and from his brother and sister, Toby smiles indiscriminately on all, while Isaac lifts up his arms to be held and Olivia complains, "When are these guys gonna learn to do things for themselves?"

Maybe my first legacy for Toby will be teaching him to do a few things for himself.

As for our Olivia, Milton has taught her to kneel, hold her arms out straight, and dive (head not belly first) neatly into a pool, his patient instruction providing her with a well-earned source of pride and a lifelong skill. My legacies for Olivia? I seem to be aspiring to a lot of them, but before she moves out I'd like to teach her ten poems, ten poems I'll try (as I tried and failed with my children) to persuade her to learn in exchange . . . for payments in cash. (I know this sounds crass, but I'm trying it anyway.) Since O is a child who has memorized vast portions of *The Incredibles, Shrek,* and *The Lion King,* I figure that she can do the same with verse, inspired by her grandmother's enthusiasm as well as by a dollar for every poem learned.

My fantasy is that someday she'll be stuck in traffic on the New Jersey Turnpike and instead of cursing her fate she'll recite a few poems, and maybe she'll think of her grandma who tucked these words into her soul when she was a child. On the other hand, if she's stuck in traffic cursing her fate instead of reciting poetry, I'm hoping she doesn't remember that her grandmother taught her a few of those curse words too. (Not on purpose, of course. Certainly not! "Oh, shit" isn't part of my intended legacy.)

Now we know what can happen to language when children dutifully learn words by heart without a full grasp of what it is they're saying. My current favorite malapropism is Nathaniel's rendition of the Pledge of Allegiance, which he recites with great precision right until he hits "one nation, under guard." (Though now that I'm thinking about it, maybe it's not a malapropism at all.)

I'm planning to teach Olivia to understand a poem's sense as well as its sound, even when the sense is sort of silly, which is why I'm starting with Lear's delicious ode to intermarriage, "The Owl and the Pussy-Cat." I'll have to explain about "five-pound notes" and "shillings" and "mince" and "quince," as well as "bong-trees." And we'll both have to learn the meaning of "runcible spoon." But I hope that O will be tickled when "Pussy, my love" gets married to "Owl," that "elegant fowl," and the two of them dance "hand in hand . . . by the light of the moon." And I hope that I can persuade this tenacious, relentless, world-class negotiator that, although—

47

yes, she's right—this poem has three verses indeed, I intend to pay her ONE dollar to learn it, not three.

O has more time to learn poetry over the weekend, when camp is out and when she, and all the rest of us, are at home, four grown-ups in charge of keeping three children happily occupied for two days and three evenings. The challenge here is to not succumb to entertaining the kids with too many sugary treats and DVDs, and every weekend we flunk this test once again. This is not a failure to play countless games or to color countless pages of coloring books or to spend countless hours at swimming pools and playgrounds or to countlessly read yet another Sendak or Seuss. Nor is this a failure to arrange for compatible play dates and jolly outings. The problem, instead, is that while Alexander will go for a ride on his bike on Saturday morning, tugging Isaac behind in his two-wheeled buggy; and while Marla, off in another direction, will go for a long sweaty run, pushing Toby ahead of her in his red jogger; and while Milton and I will summon all our energy and inventiveness to make certain that O is diverted while they are gone, when everyone's done with their biking and running and back at the house again, it still is only ten o'clock in the morning.

We of a certain age agree that time goes by faster and faster as we grow older. One of the few exceptions is spending Friday night to Sunday night with the grandchildren.

*   *   *

One Friday in late July, Alexander and Marla packed the children into the car and drove down to Rehoboth Beach for the weekend. Milton and I, with the house to ourselves, seemed hardly to know what to do, but when we had locked all the doors and turned the security system to "on" and got into bed, we figured it out. On Saturday I spent a few hours restoring our kitchen to its former orderliness. On Sunday morning we read the *Post* and the *Times* not to "Elmo's Song," but to J. S. Bach. Nothing was spilled in the course of our lunch and no sippy cups graced our table. And when I went upstairs to take a shower and shampoo my hair, I was the only person in the bathroom.

Arriving on Sunday night from the beach, Isaac beamed us a thoroughly happy "hi-yo." Toby dispensed a gurgle and a coo. Alexander and Marla pronounced the weekend a great success. And Olivia, who, along with the others, headed into the kitchen for a snack, instantly started recounting her adventures in Rehoboth at a pace somewhat faster than the speed of light.

"We saw jellyfishes. Yuck! And we saw dolphins in the ocean. Twelve of them! Awesome! And I rode on rides. And I won a frog. And built sandcastles in the sand. And I held my breath and jumped in big waves with my daddy."

Sitting at the table of my already ravaged kitchen with Toby, now in my arms, spitting up on my dress, I smiled at my sandy family and said that the weekend sounded like fun and that I was happy they'd had such a wonderful time. And then I added, surprised to find myself swept with an unexpected rush of emotion, "But Papa and I are so glad you're all back. We missed you."

CHAPTER FOUR

The Resident
Grown-Ups

"You know that big oak dresser on the third floor," I say nonchalantly to Alexander, "the one with the heavy top that sometimes unexpectedly comes crashing down . . . ?"

"If this is a conversation," he says, stopping me in my tracks, "that's going to end up with how this dresser top can crush children's little fingers, which to my mind kind of suggests that I'm not smart enough to watch out for my own kids, I don't want to hear it."

"I didn't intend to say any such thing," I instantly reply to him, in a tone combining huffiness and hurt. "I only wanted to mention that I'd be happy to take the blankets out of that dresser to give your family a bit more room for clothes."

I was lying, of course. Alexander had nailed it. And looking at me quizzically as I hastily improvised my blanket story, he knew I knew he knew that I had lied. But both of us let it ride—I deciding I wouldn't insist that he accept my story and he deciding, I guess, that a son shouldn't call his mother a liar in her own home.

Normally Alexander, when we aren't sharing a house, is a joy to be with—funny, charming, kindhearted, smart, sensitive to other people's needs, and not only my youngest son but my very good friend. Most of the time, even living here, he is all of the above except when (in his view) I'm treating him like a child, except when (always with tact, in my view) I'm issuing warnings and making helpful suggestions.

It's inevitable, I suppose, that living, as Milton and I are now living, in close quarters with our resident grown-up children, there are bound to be opportunities—many opportunities—for intergenerational irritations. Some of them, however, some of us parents might be able to avoid by repeating the following mantra twice a day:

Don't judge, advise, or criticize.

Respect their boundaries and choices.

Accept who they are.

Well, sometimes we need to repeat it *ten* times a day. And then we must try to abide by what we say. I'm doing my best.

This doesn't mean that I always succeed in keeping my mouth shut when I should keep my mouth shut. But I don't understand those parents who won't ever try. Who always feel compelled to offer their children their full and brutally frank opinion. Who insist that they have, as obviously I don't, much too much integrity to lie. Who make it blazingly clear that they don't approve of the way their children are managing money, or raising their kids, or even cutting their hair. And who haven't figured out that in order to keep the family intact, they must not mess with the mates their children have chosen. Indeed, when a friend once said to me, "What am I going to do? I really don't like the woman my son has married," I—a great believer in family intactness—had only one answer to offer: "Learn to like her."

I've happily had the good fortune to really like, to *love,* the women my sons have married. And I think that they like, maybe even love, Milton and me. These fond feelings are surely helping us through our summer's intense togetherness. In fact, with a few exceptions, the four of us seem to be living together with considerable grace and civility.

With a few exceptions.

My husband, for example, profoundly hates to throw out food. Cartons and bunches and baggies of what have clearly gone from perishables to perished languish in our refrigerator for months, growing ever smellier and moldier and limper and more repulsive while the expiration dates recede into the distant—far, far distant—past. (Our wines should be as old as some of our milk.) When Alexander or Marla cries out in horror at the color (black) of the cream cheese or the stench (words fail me) of the half-and-half, Milton mocks them for being overfastidious, pointing out that, coming from a poor family, he has learned to ignore bad smells and to cut off the black parts.

I sympathize with Marla and Alexander's concerns about poisoning the family, but explain (in private) that Milton absolutely cannot (at his age) be retrained, and that our only defense is to get rid of this sordid stuff when he's out of the house. And since he sometimes checks the trash to make sure we're not disposing of (in his view, his view only) viable food, I also advise them to camouflage, with paper towels and napkins, the monstrosities they've dumped into the trash.

The three of us are aligned against Milton on this particular issue. On another issue, however, it's three against me, with Milton and

Marla and Alexander complaining constantly that the house is too cold while I am pointing to sweat on my brow and a temperature reading of eighty-seven degrees in an effort to convince them that objectively it's intolerably hot. Whenever I enter a room I close any open windows and doors and switch on one of our twelve separate a.c. units. Whenever they enter a room they do the reverse. And when I insist that if I don't cool off the kitchen I'm going to die of heat prostration, they counter with fine, okay, and I should try not to blame myself when my grandchildren's sniffles turn into full-blown pneumonia. I don't switch on the a.c. I die of heat prostration.

This pneumonia ploy, by the way, may be the only situation in which Alexander and Marla and Milton outworry, or pretend to outworry, me, for most of the time the three of them are exuding disapproval over my constant and, to them, excessive concerns about everybody's safety.

I admit that they've learned, for the most part, the futility of telling me to stop worrying, But sometimes I think I'm the only one who cares. For they're often rolling their eyes when I'm rescuing O

 from what I'm convinced is a near-death experience, or prying from Isaac's mouth an excessive number of easy-to-choke-on gummy bears. And though Marla is always gracious when I mention a dozen symptoms that she might want to share with Toby's pediatrician, I don't think she shares.

I would also like to note that, while I'm doing all the above, I don't appreciate Milton saying to Marla and Alexander, "She can't help it."

As for the safety, health, and well-being of my resident son and daughter-in-law, I do leave a number of my concerns unexpressed, determined to show respect for the fact that in their opinion (and most of the time in mine) they're capable of taking care of themselves. This means that I won't urge Marla to go to bed instead of to work when she's suffering from a major case of flu and won't tell Alexander that, as the father of three, it's his duty to give up his perilous passion for twenty-four-hour mountain-bike racing in favor of something slower and saner, like golf.

Although I didn't talk about my mountain-bike-racing fears to Alexander, I did find occasion to bring them up with Marla, who discouraged any further exploration of the subject by noting that Alexander (a) is a sensible, responsible, excellent biker and (b) loves biking too much to be asked to relinquish it. I'm hoping she will stick by the rule that "whatever's said in the kitchen stays in the kitchen" and not mention our little chat to Alexander.

Another matter I won't discuss—nor will Milton discuss—with Alexander is an article we recently read in *Time*. It reports on the risks, to men, of sexual difficulties and "perineal pain" resulting from the pressure that bike seats put on certain sensitive parts of the body. This problem can be solved by using a nontraditional bike seat that is shrewdly designed to be "genitalia-friendly," but I don't think we'll be buying him one for his birthday. We're still giving thought, however, to—some night while he is sleeping—slipping the article under his bedroom door.

If there's anything else I might say or do, or that Milton might say or do, that might irritate Marla or Alexander or both, maybe they—like us—could try a mantra, something for those fraught moments when they feel we've crossed over the line, something to help them tolerate the incursions of the older generation, something to repeat to themselves over and over again, something like this:

They love us.

They're trying.

They mean well.

Cut them some slack.

Milton and I take credit for being at our most restrained about the religious upbringing of our grandchildren, offering not a single opinion or helpful word of advice and discovering that some-times—as the old cliché would have it—silence is golden. Let me explain:

Tony's wife, Hyla, is Jewish, but Alexander and Nick married women who are not. Years ago, back when our sons were teens, Milton and I had informed them on several occasions that, although we weren't seriously observant, we both would be pleased, would pre-fer, to have Jewish grandchildren. But when our sons brought Marya and Marla into our life, our gratitude at having such glori-ous daughters-in-law trumped our concerns about how their kids would be raised.

Both of these couples, however, without displaying the slightest need to consult with us, decided that they would raise their children as Jews.

Alexander and Marla made their decision public at Olivia's

naming ceremony, where, at a party for family and friends, Alexander gave a little speech. He said that before they had married, he and Marla—touring western and eastern Europe—had spent a day at Auschwitz confronting the grim and graphic evidence of the mass extermination of the Jews. Staggering out, they asked each other what they could do, what response they could possibly make, to what they had seen. "And we decided that what we could do," Alexander explained, "would be for us to raise Jewish children." He then thanked Marla "for joining me on this journey," while Milton—standing right behind me—soaked the entire back of my blouse with his tears.

Marya and Nick approached the Jewish question with a lot less emotion. "So I said to Nick," said Marya, "that I'm perfectly willing to bring up our children as Jews if he'll just agree to raise them as Giant fans. And Nick said, 'No, we'll bring them up as Giant *and* Redskin fans, and when they're eighteen they'll get to choose for themselves.'"

Nathaniel and Benjamin, the theology of football notwithstanding, will—it's been agreed—be raised as Jews.

Needless to say, determining what it means to "be raised as Jews" can be rather tricky, with O overheard explaining matter-of-factly to a playmate, "My daddy's Jewish and my mommy's Christmas." But yesterday she came home from camp announcing she'd just learned a new foreign language, "Oy vey." Milton and I will continue to keep our mouths shut.

*   *   *

One striking aspect of two married couples living together in the same house over time is that we become witnesses to each other's marriage. We hear each other's irritated "yes, dears." We notice each other's cold glances and stormy brows. We read the subtext of unspoken resentments. We vibrate to the urgency that's buried beneath a quiet, "I need you here—now." And if the marriage we're witnessing belongs to our very own son and daughter-in-law, we're paying more than ordinary attention.

But along with taking note of the expectable everyday tensions of married life, Milton and I are having the pleasure of seeing, day after day, what a mutually loving, respectful, modern, truly egalitarian marriage looks like. And we're giving ourselves some credit for what we see.

Just last week, in fact, when I was rinsing off some saucers and cups in the sink, Alexander walked into the kitchen and, in mock amazement, stopped dead and stared. "No offense, Mom," he said, "but I think this may be the first time in my life that I've ever actually seen you washing dishes."

He exaggerates, of course. But not by much. For when he was growing up—in a household four-fifths of which was male—the prevailing rule was Women Don't Do Dishes. And having watched his father, with equal adroitness, put on an apron and whip up breakfast, or put on a baseball mitt and field a ball, or put him to bed while I finished writing an article, he (and both of his brothers) acquired a broadened, enlightened view of what it really meant to be a man.

Now I'm not prepared to claim that Milton and I have a "truly egalitarian" marriage. But he was, from the start, more involved with the house and the kids, with the domestic side of life, than any other husband that I knew. And if he believed that women were born with a gene that, unlike men, equipped them to tolerate changing dirty diapers, there were plenty of other things he was willing to do. Well before the Women's Movement was raising men's consciousness, my husband knew that in order for our family, with three children and two working parents, to stay afloat, he had to pitch in.

Alexander does more than pitch in. He does half. And he does it without being told what he has to do. And, unlike many husbands and wives, who stake out separate realms of expertise—the daddy barbecues, the mom wipes bottoms; the daddy does playgrounds, the mom does pediatricians—both he and Marla can, and do, do it all.

Milton and I watch with awe when Marla goes straight from work to dinner with a client while Alexander takes full charge of the kids—making pasta, changing diapers, giving baths, putting on pajamas, reading separate stories to Isaac and O, providing them each with a final bottle or sippy cup or juice box, and then persuading them to go to sleep. We also watch with awe when Marla, taking pity some mornings on Alexander, lets him ride his beloved bike to his office while she, cool and polished in her size-zero suit and swept-up hair, takes full charge of some often

We MeaN WeLL

recalcitrant kids—getting them fed and dressed, and loading and locking them into the car, and then (this, of course, is during rush-hour traffic) driving first to Olivia's camp and then to Toby and Isaac's day-care center and then to her office.

Is all of this always accomplished with sweetness and light and a touch of humor and great good nature? Certainly not. There is grumpiness. Sulky silences. Frustration. And sometimes, when Marla or Alexander inquires of the other, "Are you okay?" the answer is a snarky, "Okay? Why shouldn't I be okay? You're walking out and leaving me with three children."

If Marla and Alexander have been having more ferocious exchanges than that, they obviously have been doing so out of our earshot. We've never once heard them conducting a serious fight, though Milton and I have engaged in one or two, or three or four, during their residence. But we held them behind closed doors, replacing our usual snarls and roars with hisses and whispers, sparing our children the knowledge that after forty-six years of marriage all marital conflicts may not yet be resolved. I must confess, however, that on a couple of occasions I've been tempted to get Alexander and Marla involved, tempted to offer them absolute proof of the rightness of my position and, in my closing arguments, to persuade them to convict and sentence Milton. (And maybe even award me emotional damages.) Luckily, before I went public—though justice was on my side—I got a grip on myself.

It is our observation that our son and our daughter-in-law already have a pretty good grip on themselves.

Another observation we've made about Marla and Alexander,

but it's also true of our other two sons and their wives, is that they almost always choose to socialize as a family with other families rather than ditch the children and go out on a weekend date with other couples. This lack of what, when Milton and I were the parents of young kids, we called "grown-up time," is surely due in part to economics, for what with the high price of baby-sitters and just about everything else, even a fast-food dinner and a movie can wind up costing a hundred dollars. But maybe some other reasons for the absence of grown-up time are two-career guilt and current child-rearing theories, which may be persuading parents that they can't possibly be good parents unless they spend every free moment with their children. Oh, and one more thing: We've noticed that fifteen minutes after the kids fall asleep, their exhausted parents are ready for bedtime too.

Leaving only JuJu and Papa, the wide-awake septuagenarians, ready to party.

In the second half of August, Steve and Jeannette drove down from Manhattan for a visit, upping the resident grown-ups temporarily to six and changing the balance of power to a mighty two adults for every child. Our plan was to play with the children, wear out the children, put them to bed, and then for us six to enjoy some grown-up time.

Jeannette, who started out as a friend of Nick's, has been part of our family for what seems forever, having moved here from Taiwan and living with us while she went to school, and growing so dear to our hearts that she became our sons' "almost sister" as well as an "almost daughter" to Milton and me. Although she had been in no rush, there came a time she was ready to marry, but none of the men she was meeting seemed to be what any of us considered husband material. And so I telephoned Phyllis, whom I have known since age seventeen, and asked about the status of her son Steve, and learning that he was single, unengaged, and marriage-minded, I told her she had to tell him that he had to call Jeannette immediately. There was a little resistance on Phyllis's part ("Everybody wants to fix him up") and a little resistance on Steve's part ("Do I want my *mom* and her *girlfriend* to fix me up?") and then he called. The rest, including a beaming Milton walking Jeannette down the aisle, is history.

I want to take a moment here to say that I think it's our duty—everyone's duty—to fix up single women and single men, preferably for purposes of matrimony. We who actually know them surely are better than those computer dating services at figuring out their potential compatibility, plus it's exceedingly unlikely that any person we fix up is going to turn out to be a serial killer. Fixing up women and men has its risks—"How desperate do you think I am?" "*That* was your idea of a nice human being?"—but we shouldn't be discouraged by matchmaking failures or even by matchmaking catastrophes. For eventually, like me, you may after many misses make the perfect match, turning two people—two strangers who wouldn't have met if we had minded our own business—into one quite happily married couple.

And now the happy couple is spending three nights on the floor of Milton's second-floor office, where, they insist, they sleep better—buffered by quilts and sleeping bags—than they ever do in their bed back home in New York. They are, as they always are, quite perfect houseguests.

Olivia, who's in love with her uncle Steve and her aunt Jeannette—whom she calls by her Chinese name, Aunt Ching Yi—hangs out with them every moment they're around, making only one wistful complaint: "How come they always sleep so late in the morning?" This means O is waiting impatiently, bursting with questions to ask and games to play, when they wander down to breakfast at 8:30, so eager to be in their presence that, given the choice between swimming with them or getting her ears pierced, she chooses swimming.

I sit by the pool with Toby, who's happily chomping on the fist he has stuffed in his mouth, as Olivia, with some final instructions from Milton, demonstrates her back flip for Steve and Jeannette, and Isaac is introduced to total immersion underwater in the sheltering arms of his mother and his dad. Listening to the grown-ups shouting, "Good job," and O and Isaac yelping with pleasure, while a soft breeze blows through this flawless summer day, I am full of smiles and tears at the same time, full of the difficult knowledge that I can't, as a poet once put it, "cage the minute within its nets of gold." I am achingly aware of the fragility of these fleeting sunlit moments, set as they are within a wider world of deprivation and danger and grief. And I am achingly aware of

how very little I can do (though I have to keep doing it) to try to make the world better for my children, for their children, for everyone's children.

At which point Toby produces a major poop, effectively putting a pungent end to smiles, tears, poetry, and aching awareness.

On Sunday night Alexander and Steve took complete charge of dinner from drinks to dessert, and the six of us did indeed have some grown-up time, though, having exhausted ourselves in the process of trying to wear out the children, we were ready to head to bed by ten o'clock. On Monday, Steve and Jeannette drove back to New York, and later that day I said to O, "Tell me, what was your favorite part of their visit." She thought about this for a while and then replied with a satisfied smile, "Everything."

Everyone in the house, it seemed, was satisfied with everything. But satisfaction here has a very short shelf life.

On Tuesday morning, coming down to the kitchen unusually early, I opened the door without turning off the alarm, causing it to ring out loud and long on the third floor and scaring the hell out of everybody up there. Alexander, who hates our alarm precisely because people fail to turn it off, roared with outrage from the top of the stairs, "Do you *ever* frighten bad guys with that [many expletives deleted] alarm? Or do you only frighten good guys, like us?"

All this before we even got to breakfast.

And at breakfast total chaos descended, with Isaac screaming for incomprehensible reasons and Olivia engaged in a world-class sulk and a yowling Toby repudiating his pacifier, his bottle, and his bowl of warmed rice cereal both with and without bananas and apple-sauce.

"We should have slept late today," Milton whispered to me, as we tried unsuccessfully to be helpful. "Oh, yes," I whispered back in sympathy, reminding myself that there definitely are minutes I don't want to cage within their nets of gold.

CHAPTER FIVE

Where Have All the Playpens Gone?

$\mathcal{M}$ ilton is out of town for the night and I've immediately acquired another bed partner. It's Olivia, with whom I have arranged, in my husband's absence, a sleepover date. Instead of spending the night on the third floor with her mother and father and her two brothers, she is happily snuggled underneath my quilt, having already showered with me, picked us a movie to watch, and convinced me that while we're lying here in our nighties watching *Ice Age,* we ought to be fortified with a couple of lollipops.

It is all quite cozy.

But O doesn't want me popping out of bed every now and then to do a few chores across the hall in my office. Nor does she even want me on the floor right next to the bed knocking off some crunches and some leg lifts. She expects me instead to be spending every minute at her side, watching the movie and sucking my lollipop. She expects, and she is getting, my full attention.

Meanwhile, Marla is giving Toby a bath and because he loves it so much they linger, filling the room with the sound of splashing and squeals. And Alexander wrestles with Isaac, whose current state of desperate discontent is being expressed in operatic decibels. Each of us, in other words, is occupied completely with one child, which seems to be all, at the moment, we can handle. So how do just *two* parents handle three?

How did we?

I'm convinced that raising children was much easier when Milton and I raised our children. Not easy, heaven knows, but a lot less difficult than it seems to be today. I remember, for instance, piling hordes of kids—maybe eight or nine kids—into the front, back, and way back of our small station wagon, back in those good old bad old days before the use of seat belts and car seats was mandatory. Now, however, loading and locking the children into the car strikes me as a deeply daunting experience involving, as it does, all kinds of straps that cross over and under thrashing limbs and then buckle tightly in inaccessible places. I wonder if parents of Alexander and Marla's generation register how tough it is to simply get their kids in and out of the car, though watching Milton and me as we bitch and moan and growl at each other might give them a hint. For the klutziness we demonstrate in attempting to extricate Toby from his bouncy seat is pitifully on display when we're installing him or Isaac or O in a car (and equally on display when we're removing them). Slow learners doesn't even begin to describe us.

"Please, Isaac," I'll sometimes whine, "you know where this damn—I mean, darn—strap goes, so work with me, won't you?" But Isaac, whose arm or leg or neck I'm inadvertently twisting, is usually in too much pain to help. And Olivia, when she offers assistance—"No JuJu, Papa, no! You do it like *this!*"—does so in the same exasperated tone of voice that her father uses when showing us, yet again, how to set the clock on our TV. Not surprisingly, Milton and I, when we're baby-sitting our grandchildren, avoid—whenever possible—going anywhere we can't get to on foot.

We acknowledge, of course, that car seats save children from injury and death and recognize, though we grumble, their necessity. But when it comes to another basic change in child-care equipment—the disappearance, the banishment, of the playpen—we simply cannot fathom why the parents of young children have permitted this.

We need a national Bring Back the Playpen movement. I've already written lyrics for a "Where Have All the Playpens Gone?" national song. Milton and I reject the misguided argument that playpens are cages for children (though cages are where certain children we've met belong). And though it's too late for Isaac and O, we'd like to succeed in bringing back the playpen in time for Toby and all the significant grown-ups in his life to reap its benefits. Which are, as Milton and I recall from our days as the grateful parents of playpenned children, as follows:

The playpen provides a clean, well-lighted place, a small room of one's own, where a crawling child can be—from time to time in the course of a day—safely and, we insist, happily deposited. Equipped with toys, stuffed animals, and other entertainments, the playpen enables a child to play, explore, practice standing and sitting, examine the world without encountering possibly fatal temptations and thus without having to hear a prohibiting "Stop!" or "Get away from that!" or "No!" Ensconced in his own private space, he learns to entertain and even to soothe himself while the grown-ups, unencumbered, eat a meal, make a bed, do the dishes, read a newspaper, and even go to the bathroom all by themselves. Indeed, I'd like to recommend as the motto of this Bring Back the Playpen movement, a stirring Free to Pee—Not You, Just Me.

There are those who'll undoubtedly argue that my advocacy of the playpen is actually a form of child abuse, a callous disregard for the needs of a child to either roam freely or—even more important—to be carried, held, steadfastly attached. But while I recognize the mutual gratification of holding and being held, the glued-to-each-other parenting that I see in some families today strikes me as Attachment Theory run wild. For surely we should be able to provide a steady, secure, and loving connection without insisting it's necessary to constantly carry and sleep with and date our child. And surely, although I will never succeed in converting the true believers, there must be plenty of sensible parents around, parents like Alexander and Marla, who don't seem to overdo the attachment thing and who just need to be convinced that they will have much easier lives if we BRING BACK THE PLAYPEN.

I think that another reason why my friends and I had an easier time raising children is that many, many more parents today consider it unacceptable to let their children cry themselves to sleep. They sit with their kids, they hold their hands, they stretch out and snuggle with them, and they take them—if all else fails, and sometimes well before all else fails—into their beds, insisting they can't let their children lie there feeling lonely and frightened and abandoned, and citing other cultures where everybody in the family sleeps together.

The parents of my generation, at least the parents that I knew, did not do this.

"You just let them cry?" a young mother asked me, sounding so appalled that I wondered if she was planning to report me retroactively to the Children's Protective Services of D.C. "You let them keep crying? How could you be so hard-hearted?"

But those of us who were bringing up our children back then were certainly not hardhearted, content to let them suffer while we selfishly indulged in fun and games. We tucked them in and read them books and brought them a glass, or two, or three of water before declaring that sleep time was starting right now. And if, after that, we hung tough, refusing to rush to their room when we heard their calls and cries, we restrained ourselves on the grounds that it was important to their development to learn to fall asleep at night unaccompanied.

I'm not even claiming that my way is the only right way for parents to handle bedtime. In fact, I do know children who, having spent their first few years either in their parents' bed or with their mother or father sleeping in theirs, have moved without hassle to falling asleep on their own. But I strongly believed, and my friends believed, and I guess I still believe, that the nonnegotiable, each-in-his-own-bed bedtime is going to be, in the long run, good for our children. And I strongly believe that the nonnegotiable bedtime made raising children easier for us.

*   *   *

Raising kids was certainly also much easier back in our day than right now because these days parents seem to feel they're always obliged to explain themselves to their kids while we parents felt allowed—I guess there's no nice way to say this—to be more fascistic. While Toby this morning is wearing a little cute bib unabashedly lettered Benevolent Dictator, the benevolent dictators during the time of our young parenthood were Milton and me. This means we often replied, after we'd told a child to "Do it," and he, instead of doing it, asked "Why?" with a simple, end-of-discussion, "Because we said so." And if some child complained that *we* were doing something we'd said *he* couldn't do, we never once hesitated pointing out to him, "That's because we're the grown-ups and you're the kid."

Again, Alexander and Marla almost never overdo the overexplaining thing, but we see many parents spending—wasting—enormous chunks of time trying to justify their requests and their limit-setting. Like interminably explaining why it's not a great idea to draw on the living-room wall with Mommy's lipstick. Like repeatedly suggesting that maybe she ought to let Daddy help her pour the milk since she's missing the bowl and pouring the milk on the table. Like patiently documenting, perhaps with a few citations from the Geneva Conventions, some of the reasons why he might consider removing his foot from his brother's face. Now don't get me wrong: I believe there are times when sitting down with a child to carefully explain why this is expected and that is forbidden can help that child to decide for himself or herself to make the decision to do the right thing. But back in those harried days when I needed Nick, my most challenging son, to stop with his forty reasons why he found it absurd to be asked to wear his rain boots, the only way I could get three children out of the house and into the car pool on time was to say, "Enough now. Just put on the boots."

Calling on my inner fascist on a regular basis made parenthood easier. So did—and here's another chance to accuse me of child abuse—the judiciously and appropriately applied smack. I don't think I ever hesitated to give my children a smack when I thought they needed one, especially when they let go of my hand and ran out into the street right in front of a truck. But almost all the parents of my children's generation seem to strongly disapprove of smacking, arguing, and they probably do have a point here, that violence of any kind will beget violence. Nevertheless I found the smack, in certain fraught situations, more effective and more efficient than either a conversation or go-to-your-room Time Out, which is probably the most popular tactic these days for conveying parental disapproval. Indeed, I sometimes wonder about the effectiveness of Time Outs, recalling the little girl who, being told that her time was up and she could come back now, replied she was having so much fun playing alone in her room that could she please stay there just a little bit longer.

Actually, Nick's wife, Marya, who very strongly doesn't believe in smacking, but who sometimes finds that Time Out doesn't quite do the job, has come up with what I regard as a clever technique for disciplining a wayward child. When Nathaniel, for instance, is persecuting his little brother Benjamin, Marya warns him a couple of times to stop, adding the second time around that if he doesn't stop, "There will be consequences." Nathaniel, who, with great passion, has told his mother on many occasions, "I hate consequences," may nonetheless find it difficult to stop. And then his mother takes away a toy that he is fond of and puts it in the basement of their apartment building, where it will soon be acquired by another—and, we hope, more virtuous—child.

As a grandma who almost always defers to the child-raising rules of her sons and daughters-in-law, I have given up smacks and rely on Time Outs and consequences. But I still believe that dispensing with the occasional whack on the back of a hand or a backside may make it a little harder today to raise kids.

And another thing: Parents today seem to feel more compelled than I or my friends ever did to enrich their children extracurricularly, committed to transporting them after school and/or on weekends to a smorgasbord of life-enhancing activities. These deliveries and

pickups, time-consuming and usually hectic, were of course also going on in my child-raising days, with plenty of parents (mostly female parents) routinely schlepping their children to piano, karate, ice-skating, drawing, ballet, and the occasional mother driving her daughter twice a week, every week, an hour each way, because of that daughter's love affair with a horse. Even *I* spent one full year chauffeuring Nick to a Saturday-morning art class under the delusion that he might be the next Michelangelo or Paul Klee. But after that year, I decided that my children could take whatever lessons they wanted only when they were old enough to get to that lesson by riding on a bus.

And although I think that my friends and I tried to provide our children with assorted developmental opportunities, I don't believe we perceived them as necessities, necessities without which they would be hindered in their climb from preschool to Harvard, necessities without which they would surely be lacking a competitive edge. But more and more parents today, in the hopes of helping their children surge to the head of the pack, are signing them up, ever earlier, for another and yet another enriching activity, urging them to keep practicing, pushing them to excel, engaging in what has aptly been called "hyperparenting."

With their Spanish lessons, swimming lessons, soccer practice, a class called Music for Aardvarks, our various grandchildren have certainly not been deprived. On the other hand, they have not been hyperparented. But surely the pressure that many mothers and fathers feel today are making them spend more energy and time to pump up their kids than they can afford. Surely the pressure they seem to feel to burnish, before age two, their children's CV makes it a lot harder to bring up their children.

*   *   *

79

Maybe it's also harder because today's children seem to grow up faster and smarter, picking up information at a considerably earlier age and demanding immediate answers to difficult questions. Not that the parents of my generation didn't have to deal with difficult questions. But I don't think we felt compelled to be quite as dutiful and detailed in our replies.

I'll never forget the day that I was navigating our car through rush-hour traffic when Nick, age six or seven, gave me a poke on my upper arm and asked, "What's the difference between a Jew and a Christian?" Feeling a little tense from running late and low on gas, not to mention that traffic, I wanted to terminate this discussion fast. "Christians believe that Jesus Christ is the savior of mankind," I told him. "And Jews believe that he's just a regular person."

Nick sat in silence a little while, pondering the wisdom of my reply, and then he poked my arm again and asked, "So you're saying that right when I was born, already I decided inside my head that Jesus Christ was *not* the savior of mankind?"

To which I replied, "Shut up, Nick. I'm driving."

Am I proud of this? No, I'm not. Would mothers today respond this way? I think not. Indeed I am convinced that if there were a bumper sticker proclaiming WE BRAKE FOR THEOLOGICAL AND OTHER QUESTIONS, most young parents would paste it onto their car. At the very least they'd all say, "Excellent question!"

Many kids' questions arise from the fact that they're living in a far more perilous world than the world in which my friends and I raised our children. As a result they require a lot more guidance from their parents in sorting out what they hear—too much, too soon—

about drugs, AIDS, pedophilia, and terrorism. Nathaniel was only four when his preschool teacher announced to his class that, by order of the New York Board of Education, they were going to have a Drug-Free Week, part of which involved having the students stand up and recite an "I'm drug-free" pledge. Arriving home and declaring, "I told the flag I'm drug-free, Mommy," Nathaniel then required some clarification of exactly what it was he was talking about.

He also needed to understand, on the fifth anniversary of 9/11, when stories about the event were inescapable, why the two towers fell down and if the planes that crashed into the towers made a mistake and if it wasn't an accident who were the bad guys. Marya, who on that harrowing day was over eight months pregnant with Nathaniel and on her way to her office in the South Tower, explains to me, "I didn't want to tell him but he asked and I kind of froze and my feeble brain could manage to come up with just one thing—the truth."

Someday I'll show Nathaniel a special message tacked on that bulletin board in my office. It's an e-mail from his mother, dated 9/11/01, and the time is 2:23:48 p.m., the time when Milton and I, quietly weeping in front of the television set and waiting for our telephone to ring, finally received her vastly relieving words, "Have been trying to call you but can't get through. I am exhausted and sad, but grateful I wasn't hurt and that, as far as I know, my colleagues are O.K." Someday I'll show him that message but for the moment his mother has hastened to reassure him that he shouldn't brood about future 9/11s, that "we'll do everything we can to keep you safe."

Hyla, my Denver daughter-in-law, also wants to keep her children safe but she does not intend to inform her seven-year-old about pedophiles who kidnap, rape, and murder. She was, however, concerned about curbing Bryce's risky habit of wandering out of her sight in public places like the supermarket or playground. Her solution has been to persuade him that he needs to stay close to her side, "because people who want to have children but can't may sometimes take other people's children home with them." Although she omitted the horror stories underlying her warning—and there certainly seem to be more of them these days—she succeeded in making Bryce a bit more cautious and more fearful as, regretfully, he maybe needs to be.

Tony has had to alert Bryce's sister Miranda, age eleven, to dangers that didn't exist when he was her age—the dangers lurking in cyberspace for an innocent young kid with an e-mail address. Miranda has been told to never agree to meet someone who shows up on her computer screen, a someone who may sound like a way-cool girlfriend but in fact could be a grown man with bad intentions. And although she might not yet know or understand a term like "sexual predator," she is now well aware that things may not be what they seem.

 As for O, her concerns at the moment are still restricted to issues that Milton and I addressed with our own three sons, familiar issues like where do babies come from, does everyone die, is there a God. In a recent chat with her mom, Olivia scoffed at the notion

that humans evolved from monkeys, insisting not only that God had created man on the sixth day but also that, on the third day, He had created rivers and trees and "all the sidewalks." Her parents, however, know that any minute now they'll be having talks with O about some of the tough contemporary matters that some of her cousins are already dealing with.

In a world where the morning papers and nightly news shows, with urgent words and vivid pictures, bring into every home the latest abduction or suicide bombing or schoolhouse massacre; in a world where two-year-old Benjamin is singing (along with a song he hears on the radio) that it's "hard out here for a pimp/ . . . tryin' to get the money for the rent"; in a world where, taking a stroll with Miranda in a Denver mall, we pass a sweet-faced teenage girl whose T-shirt reads OVERWORKED AND UNDERFUCKED, children today are going to be exposed to confusing bits and pieces of awfulness, to far more information than my sons were barraged with when they were little boys. Their parents will have to provide some explanations and some answers about matters they wish their children had never heard of. In this world of TMI—too much information, too much difficult information—parents may find it harder to raise their kids.

Toby, out of the bathtub and into pajamas, is sleeping deeply in his crib now. Isaac, soothed by some stories from his daddy, has surrendered to slumber in his big-boy bed. And Olivia, our movie done, is fighting to stay awake as she lies beside me, three pillows propping up her curly head and her eyelids closing, then opening as she groggily fixes her gaze on my upper arms.

"How come you've got those wrinkles there?" she asks me.

"What are you talking about?" My voice is cold.

She points to what, despite my ardent efforts at pumping iron, could be called wrinkles.

I briskly reply, "I guess because I'm old."

"Does that mean you'll be dying soon?" she asks me.

Why am I letting this child sleep in my room?

"No," I firmly, very firmly, tell her. "No, it definitely won't be soon."

At which point O, exhausted by this profound discussion of aging and mortality, falls fast asleep.

After which I give her a kiss and—what can a grandmother do?—I burst out laughing.

CHAPTER SIX

Other Voices, Other Rooms

*B*efore the Alexander Five moved into our house for the summer, they considered renting a house of their own instead. "You can't do that!" I protested when Alexander mentioned this alternate plan on the phone. "I'm going to write a book about this experience."

On the other end of the phone I heard—dead silence. I waited. The dead silence went on, and on. "Are you still there?" I finally said, and Alexander replied: "You're planning to write about us? You're writing a book about us? And you're not even asking us if that's okay?"

On my end of the phone there was—dead silence. I was shocked into silence by what he had to say. I had spent almost all my professional life writing about my family. And I'd never asked for permission along the way. I finally found my voice: "But I have always," I told him, "written about my children." To which Alexander quietly replied, "Mom, we aren't children anymore."

A number of follow-up conversations ensued.

We eventually agreed that though he and Marla had the right to not be written about, I'd write the book, they would read it, and if (without censoring it) they gave me permission to publish it, then and only then would I try to publish it. As I'm tapping out these sentences I still don't know what their final word will be.

Meanwhile, I decided that I'd acquire a little perspective by talking to people who've done what we are doing, people who had invited (or allowed) their grown children and grandchildren to live with them. Finding families who'd been involved in these three-generation living arrangements turned out to be a lot easier than I'd expected.

Grown kids (and their kids) moved in with their parents because they were switching jobs or looking for jobs, or renovating a house or trying to find an affordable house, or saving up money. Some stayed a few weeks; some stayed for well over a year. All of the families I talked with survived the challenges of living under one roof, and everyone is still speaking to everyone else. But while some sailed smoothly through days and weeks and months of intensive togetherness, others have had a significant number of . . . issues.

These issues sometimes arose over differing expectations or personal habits or child-raising theories. These issues sometimes arose because when grown children move back home, their relationships with their parents are subject to change. And these issues sometimes arose as a result of the inescapable reality that some family members are going to be less accommodating, less adaptable, and significantly less lovable than others.

Surely one big reason why things are working out well with the Alexander Five is that all of them—five for five—are so easy to love.

*   *   *

But "lovable" is not a word that would ever cross Allison's lips when describing the three weeks, the "truly interminable" three weeks, she has just finished spending (or, as she puts it, "enduring") with her younger son, his wife, Gayle, and their "spoiled rotten" daughters, four and nine, who—while her son was in between jobs and Gayle was on vacation—came up to stay at her summer place in Maine.

Gayle, who works long hours at a high-priced, high-profile advertising agency, feels guilty, according to Allison, about having so little time to be with her girls. As a result, when she's with them, their time together must be wonderful, wonderful, wonderful, which translates, Allison says, into "no limits, nothing expected, nothing denied." They never say "thank you"; they call their parents rude names; they eat whatever, whenever, wherever they please. And, as Allison documents, they respond to even the smallest disappointment by throwing extremely loud and lingering tantrums.

"You cut my toast in squares and I wanted triangles."

Gayle says she's sorry and toasts a new piece of bread.

It isn't as good as the first piece. Daughter has tantrum.

"I told you my yellow sweater and you brought me this stupid ugly striped one instead."

Gayle says she's sorry, runs upstairs, and brings down the yellow sweater.

Too little and too late. Daughter has tantrum.

"You promised we'd go on a picnic today, but it's raining and now we can't."

Gayle says she's sorry for making it rain and proposes an indoor picnic.

Both daughters have tantrums.

Though Allison has long been aware of Gayle's permissiveness and her granddaughters' brattiness, she had never before been exposed to twenty-one days of what seemed to her—and sounds to me—like a cross between *Lord of the Flies* and Sartre's *No Exit*. During this time, however, she expressed almost no disapproval because, she explains, "It wouldn't be warmly received." She also says, "I wouldn't admit this to everyone. But I really don't love—I don't even like—my grandchildren."

Allison says she managed to remain sane and nonconfrontational because she kept her eyes on the prize—family peace; and because she kept reminding herself that in three weeks . . . two weeks . . . one week she would be rid of them; and because she kept phoning her women friends to wail into their sympathetic ears, "You'll never believe what Gayle let the kids do today." She is hoping that now that the families are living apart and on opposite coasts, distance will restore her grandmotherly feelings. But she says she won't be sharing her house with her son, his wife, and their children anytime soon. Or in the foreseeable future. Or maybe ever.

Allison's is by far the worst of the stories I've been hearing about various three-generational living arrangements. Sharon's is definitely among the best, especially when you consider that she and her husband spent an astonishing seventeen months opening their house to their son and daughter-in-law, both of them radiologists, and their three little grandchildren, plus a sleep-in nanny. This household of six has just recently returned to their own home, following the completion of an ambitious renovation that lasted twice as long as had been expected.

Getting the chance to "really know" her daughter-in-law, drinking a morning coffee with her son, being greeted at night by a joyful, "Sharie is home! Sharie is home!" from her grandchildren, Sharon says she loved virtually every minute of the time they spent together. And although she grants that "seventeen months less three days" is a significant spell of togetherness, she says there are many good reasons why it went smoothly.

She explains that, unlike Milton and me, neither she nor her husband works at home, and that they tend to dine out several nights of the week, and that along with the nanny there was also a full-time housekeeper as well as a lady who came to clean every Tuesday, and that they had a country house where she and her husband retreated, alone, many weekends. Plus, "I never changed a diaper, I never drove a car pool, I never had any real responsibility."

With a lot of paid help and their often separate routines, the two families managed to do very well together. But Sharon points out that one important secret of their success was that these arrangements didn't have to work, that if things didn't seem to be going too great, her son and his wife and his family—without any rancor—would find themselves a place to rent, and move out. "We just would have kissed them," says Sharon, "and said good-bye."

91

I am dazzled by Sharon's attitude. So mature! So self-possessed! So . . . unimaginable. Just thinking about it, I'm breaking into a sweat. Because if, God forbid, our living arrangements start unraveling and if, God forbid, it's decided—either by us or by the Alexander Five—that it would be better for all if they moved somewhere else, their moving out (no matter how lacking in rancor) would (in my opinion) prove to me and to the world that I was an utter failure as a grandmother, mother, and mother-in-law, as well as a woman and hostess and human being.

Sharon, however, experienced no such angst. Nor did she experience any difficulties. Now that her family is gone, she says, there may be some floors to refinish, some furniture to recover, some rooms to repaint, but such repairs belong in the no-big-deal category. The only real mishap that she can recall has to do with the leftovers scraped from everyone's dinner plates and stored in a plastic container for her two dogs and devoured instead by her son when he came home from work that evening, late and hungry. "My son ate the dog food," she cheerfully says. No big deal.

Another reason, says Sharon, that the house-sharing went so well was that all the adults respected each other's boundaries, accepting the fact that each family unit needed, although (or because) they were living together, plenty of opportunities for separateness. In other such households, however, that respect and acceptance were sometimes harder to come by.

One woman I talked with admits that her feelings were always being hurt when her children took her grandchildren out for pizza and a movie and didn't invite her. And another woman had already grabbed her jacket and her purse before it became quite clear to her, as her kids and their kids were heading out the door, that no one had actually asked her to come along. After hearing these women's stories I've been uneasily recalling a couple of evenings when Alexander and Marla, all their children finally asleep, sat in our kitchen chatting and drinking a beer. And then I'd walk in with Milton, and without (now that I'm thinking about it) being in any way encouraged to do so, we'd sit ourselves down and join their (now that I'm thinking about it) private conversation. Sorry, guys.

While different grandparents have differed in how to handle the issue of sufficient separateness, every one of us took the same "don't look, don't see" position regarding the quarters our children and grandchildren occupied. Top floor, basement, wherever they were located, we all agreed that the state of the rooms in which our families slept and stored their stuff was best—for the sake of our psyches and maybe even our digestions—left unviewed. I'm told that one fastidious woman, ignoring this sensible rule and opening a few doors she should never have opened, almost collapsed with shock before she fled the premises screaming, "The horror! The horror!"

Okay, so perhaps there's a little creative exaggeration here. But just a little.

What I've usually heard from women who, like me, have housed their children and their grandchildren, was that the issue of messiness only became a big problem when it took over—when, in other words, the mess had migrated out of the visiting family's sleeping quarters and started expanding throughout the rest of the house. I've been noticing that whenever the matter of this expanding messiness is discussed, some heartfelt variation of the phrase, "It made me crazy," occurs with great frequency. In Susan's case it continues to make her crazy.

"I look around," says Sue, "and the kids are dumping their things in the hall, and tossing their things on the chairs, and throwing their things on the rug, and putting their drinking glasses down on the nearest available table and just leaving them there. And they're all, their parents included, completely oblivious."

Sue also says, "If it was my daughter staying here, I wouldn't be having a problem saying, 'Pick up!' But I'm careful, very careful, about what I say to my daughter-in-law. I'm scared not to be careful."

So why doesn't Sue complain to her son? I already know the answer. Because she's convinced (and she's right) that when he gets into bed that night he will tell his wife, and that then his wife (no matter how nicely it's put) will feel she's been viciously attacked, and that then she'll deeply resent (and maybe never forgive) her mother-in-law for sneaking behind her back and saying bad things about her, and . . . And Sue, like long-suffering Allison, wants to keep peace in the family, which she won't if there is trouble with her daughter-in-law. Instead, she has decided that since the family will only be there for a couple of months, she will shut up—and pick up.

Because I don't have daughters I can't tell if I'd treat them differently from my daughters-in-law on the grounds that, as one woman put it, "I've bossed them around their entire lives and they are used to it." Isabel, however, has never developed the habit of suffering in silence, especially during the year that she and her husband shared their house with their newly divorced daughter, Wendy, and her twin sons.

That year was a tough one for Isabel because, unlike Alexander, who insists on his adult prerogatives and firmly resists my motherly ministrations, Wendy was all too eager to be taken care of. "She was trying to build up a nest egg so she could get a place of her own," Isabel tells me. "This meant she was working at a couple of jobs." And because she was running from job to job it fell to Isabel (who still worked full-time) and her husband (who had recently retired) to cook, clean, do the laundry, drive the car pool, help with the homework—deal with everything.

"My daughter was a spoiled only child, and as soon as she came back home, she wanted to be a spoiled only child again. I know she was working hard but I thought she could have helped more than she did with the kids and the housework." She let Wendy know what she thought, but nothing much changed.

Then one day Isabel lost it. "Am I going to have to die," she asked her daughter, "before you finally get your act together?" Wendy, who—without rancor, I'm told—soon thereafter moved to her own apartment, seems to be finally getting her act together.

"I'm proud of her," says Isabel, then adds, "and I was glad to see her go."

*   *   *

Audrey, a widow, would also be glad if her daughter and her daughter's family would go, but unless she gives them a shove it's unlikely to happen. For their original two-month stay has expanded into a year and a half and is looking a lot like a permanent arrangement. It's not that her house can't accommodate this extra family of three, including a son-in-law whose start-up business seems to be starting up very slowly and an almost-five-year-old granddaughter Audrey adores. But Audrey isn't quite sure if she's simply being a loving, supportive mother or what one of her friends is calling an "enabler," as in enabling her daughter—who could be working and earning some money, enough to help to pay for a place of their own—to instead take this and that and the other course in graduate school while deciding what to be when she grows up.

In addition to the enabler issue—which Audrey would never discuss with a daughter she says is "sensitive to rejection"—Audrey has the issue of her beau, a serious beau who has long been ready to move into Audrey's house, but only if the daughter and family move out. Audrey has come to realize that the only way they'll move out is if she asks them to, though she frets, "What will they do if I pull the plug?" Nevertheless, she is bracing herself to suggest that they think about making other arrangements, though she fears that this conversation, because of her daughter's sensitivity, will not go well. She is also bracing herself for some bad-mother guilt.

Another woman wonders whether perhaps she should have been more attentive and helpful during the months her son and his family were living with her. Her daughter-in-law's own mother lives abroad and rarely comes to the States to visit, but "I know she is convinced that if her mother lived near by she'd be the most devoted, perfect grandmother. I guess she was hoping that that's what I'd be, but I wasn't—I was always disappointing her." And, she adds, "I was always feeling guilty."

When you're dealing with children and grandchildren there are always opportunities to feel guilty.

The main thing I'm feeling guilty about, during this time with the Alexander Five, is that we've never yet offered—and we probably never will—to take care of all three grandchildren simultaneously. We thought we would. We intended to. We imagined saying to Marla and Alexander, "We're here, and we're staying home tonight. Go out to dinner. We'll baby-sit the kids." But instead, I'm sorry to say, each time we're on the verge of proffering our services, we remember there's three of them and just two of us. So while we're willing to baby-sit, in any combination, two out of any three of the resident grandchildren, we can't seem to find the courage to take on all of them.

But now that I'm turning my thoughts toward guilt, I'm comparing myself to a couple named Eric and Margaret. And I'm thinking that, compared to them, I probably am guilty of insufficiently loving my children and grandchildren.

For, as Eric explains it, when their daughter and her husband left Atlanta and came with their two children to live with him and his wife in Arlington, Virginia, everyone was comfortable with the fact that this was an open-ended stay, comfortable with the fact that it might take them several months before they found interesting work and affordable housing. But after Nora and Randy had finally settled into good jobs, and after half a year of remarkably easy and satisfying two-household togetherness, all of the grown-ups agreed that they wished to keep on doing what they were doing—indefinitely. Or, as Eric puts it, "Margaret and I would have been truly disappointed if Nora and Randy had wanted to move out."

As I think I've already made clear, I too would certainly be disappointed—indeed humiliated—if Alexander and Marla packed up our grandchildren and their stuff and decided to move out of our house prematurely. But Eric, setting a far higher standard for familial harmony, was telling me that he and Margaret didn't want their family moving out ever. Nor, it seems, in the year since they have made this two-household living arrangement permanent, has he or Margaret or Nora or Randy showed the slightest sign of changing their minds.

Indeed, these two married couples, plus a now four-year-old and a six-year-old, are delighted with their extended-family unit, sharing a kitchen and living room, eating most of their breakfasts and dinners together, and dividing up the cooking and cleaning and shopping and other chores—as well as each couple's financial obligations—with what I've been assured is zero acrimony.

"We all like being together," says Eric. "We all like connecting on a regular basis. We call what we're doing our PIGL, our Project for Intergenerational Living."

Why is this working? I ask. Eric replies that he and Margaret are quite tolerant of "the chaos and confusion" that accompanies their two-family living venture. He tells me that he's always been—and that Margaret now feels this way too—an "enthusiastic extended-family person, welcoming it, reveling in it, convinced that this is the way life ought to be." He also concedes that a lot of folks, including some very good friends, think that he's nuts.

I might be among the folks who think that he's nuts. On the other hand, I might have to conclude that he's just a far far finer person than I.

Whose house is it? I ask. Eric replies that he and Margaret are the owners, "but we try to make them feel that it's their house too." Who raises the kids? I ask. Eric replies that Nora and Randy are raising the children, "and we don't comment or tell them what to do." How much freedom, I ask, have you relinquished? "No more," he says, "than we're willing to give up." And what about control? I ask. Don't conflicts ever erupt over who calls the shots or which paintings should hang on the walls? The answer he gives me is hovering between rarely and not at all. For it seems that none of the four of them—in contrast, for instance, to me—is struggling much with issues of control.

I'm feeling humbled. I'm feeling inadequate. And because, as I think about it, it's becoming increasingly clear that I'll never be as generous, tolerant, openhearted, or nice as Eric and Margaret, I definitely am also feeling guilty. For though Milton and I are happy—are, in fact, thrilled—to have this precious opportunity to share our house with the Alexander Five, a big part of what makes us happy and thrilled is that this two-family living arrangement is temporary.

But before I get any guiltier, I probably ought to remind myself that Marla and Alexander want to move out of here as quickly as they can. Like us, they view this living arrangement as temporary. Like us, they aren't into overdoing this extended-family thing. Like us, though they doubtless appreciate the pleasures that sharing a household together can bring, they're also prepared to say, "Enough already." They want their own space. They want their own stuff. They want their own routine. They want to decide which paintings should hang on the walls. Maybe they want to show up for breakfast in their underwear. Maybe they want to show up in nothing at all. But whatever they want, and no matter how well our arrangements seem to be working, they have no wish to prolong any longer than absolutely necessary our adventures in intergenerational living.

And much as we adore them (and much as both of us want to believe that they adore us) we would like them to know that this doesn't hurt our feelings.

CHAPTER SEVEN

They've Left!

*E*arly in September, Milton and I took off for a seventeen-day vacation, leaving the Alexander Five still in residence. Though their renovation would not yet be done by the time of our return, it would, they assured us, be done enough. This meant that they would be moving out just before we arrived. And this meant—was this good news or bad news?—that we would be coming home to an empty house.

It was good news and bad news.

The good news, of course, was the termination of our three-story nursery school and the repossession of our grown-up life: The restoring of breakables to their former locations. The filling up of vases with water and flowers. The removal from every surface of left-behind diapers. The banishing of chaos from every shelf. And the revival of dignified dining, with background music, place mats, and adult conversation.

These mornings Milton and I can be found in the kitchen sipping our coffee and reading the papers, with only the headlines disturbing our digestion. These evenings Milton and I can be found in the kitchen sipping Shiraz and quietly chatting, with only one two three four telephone solicitations disturbing our peace. (I'm holding a little contest for the best response to these pesty solicitations, with outright rudeness prohibited and extra credit given for brevity. The current front-runner: "Thanks for calling. Bye-bye.") Here in our kitchen no one is whining or screaming or chewing on something, then spitting it out. No one is yelling, "Yuck!" or "Gross!" or "Ewwww!" Nor is anyone singing a newly learned Indian Rain Dance song—"Yo yo yo yo yo. Ya ya. Yeh yeh"—repeatedly and at the top of her lungs.

The good news is that our life is back to civilized.

The bad news is that sometimes it feels too damn civilized.

The bad news is that sometimes—no, often—we miss the mess and the noisiness of living together, entangled, side by side and cheek by jowl and tush by tush, with our boisterous, beloved Alexander Five.

Now that they've gone is everything here the way it used to be? Well, not exactly. Our house, which always looked lived in, is looking significantly more lived in, and while even the velvet has managed to survive, certain stains suggest that my wine-velvet chair has had some illicit encounters with chocolate. Our marriage has also survived, has indeed been enriched by our shared delight in our resident family, despite the fact that their presence has interfered with the marital option of running naked from room to room flinging champagne and caviar at each other before falling into a passionate heap on the floor. As for my personal growth, I ought to be modest and leave this to others to describe. On the other hand,

I'm going to do it myself on the grounds that I don't want to take any chances.

I think I'm a better person for having had this familial experience but I wouldn't say that I'm a *different* person. I'm better because, while they lived here with us, I laughed more and grumbled less. I tried not to offer too much uninvited advice. I never once suggested that the food that Isaac and O were dribbling everywhere could doubtless explain our recent influx of mice. And when I called attention to what, in my view, were endangered-grandchildren situations, I did my very best to speak in tones of calm concern, not panicked shrieks.

I'm better for knowing I could, if I had to, display more self-restraint than I ever dreamed I was capable of displaying, even though—when Isaac ran into the street outside his house after moving back home—I definitely reverted to panicked shrieks.

I'm also better for knowing that, in matters of timing and schedules, I could hang—if I had no choice—a whole lot looser, accepting the fact, for instance, that I couldn't keep writing the article I was writing because Isaac or O needed extra attention right now, accepting the fact that I'd never know before we actually sat down at the table how many people I would be feeding that night, accepting the fact that, even though I desperately wanted and needed to leave *this minute,* I couldn't until I had found one of Toby's pacifiers, accepting the fact that as long as these kids were embedded in my life, my life would be a lot more unpredictable.

Yes, while they were here I learned that I could live, if I had to live, with the unpredictable. But now that they've left I'm back to my old routines. For the fact is that I'm happier—and I always will be happier—when I'm able, unimpeded, to plan ahead. This means not only making lists of what I am going to do on a daily and weekly and monthly and—yes!—yearly basis but also always allowing myself substantial amounts of time in which to do it. I set the table for dinner parties three full days in advance. I show up at dinner parties well before my hostesses have finished dressing. I get to movies early enough to have my pick of any seat in the theater. And I also arrive at airports so far in advance of what the current guidelines require that I could forget my picture ID, go back to my house to retrieve it, and still be in the security line two hours before my plane is due to depart. This is the woman I used to be, and the woman I am today, though I actually did—for one brief shining moment—manage to tolerate the unpredictable.

I also managed to tolerate, because there was no alternative, levels of disorder that I thought I couldn't possibly abide. I mean, while I may not be the *cleanest* person in the world, the serenity of my soul requires neatness, and if I was someone given to displaying framed needlepoint epigrams on the wall, mine would unabashedly read, "A place for everything and everything in its place." But while my grandchildren lived in this house—even with their parents, ever vigilant, ever diligent, picking up after them—disorder was the order of the day, and the answer to what's a three-letter word describing the state of our household would be "sty."

To fully grasp what a great psychic leap it was for a person like me to live, day after day, in a messy house, you will have to be told about my second-floor linen closet, a confession I regard as both embarrassing and revelatory, a confession I'm hoping won't be held against me.

For I am a woman whose five big shelves in my linen closet display, along with the linens, assorted pharmaceutical supplies—Band-Aids and cough drops and toilet paper, Pepto-Bismol and nail polish and shampoo, disposable razors and Tylenol and toothpaste—all of which have been organized, have been lovingly, carefully organized, into groups. Each of these groups has then been lined up in front of a handsome blue-bordered stick-on label on which, in my best printing, I have inscribed: "cuts and bruises," "colds and vitamins," "shaving," "hair," and "teeth," and—in a burst of inspired alliteration—"bowels," "belly," and "beauty." Not everyone—I'm not naming names—during the stay of the Alexander Five had been as committed as I to keeping all items in their clearly labeled locations. But during that time I never once complained, though I did, when no one was looking, move some misplaced tubes of Crest from "belly" to "teeth," and some razors from "colds and vitamins" to "shaving." I mostly, however, managed to ignore the frequent assaults on my linen closet. My ability to silently endure the rape of my shelves was not an inconsiderable achievement.

"Why does it always have to be neat?" Olivia once inquired during her stay with us, as she played with the jewelry in my jewelry box, mixing up the pearl with the silver earrings, mixing up the necklaces with the bracelets, mixing up the rings and the pins with the earrings and the necklaces and the bracelets, until the separate sections—with a place for everything, everything in its place—were indistinguishable.

"Because I like it like that," I said, removing a glittery choker from her grasp and returning it to where the chokers belonged, prepared to insist on my absolute right to retain a few remaining enclaves of orderliness. But then she reached out and stroked it, saying, "It's so beauty-full, JuJu. Can't I just hold it?" tilting her head in her irresistible way and making me feel like one of those terrible people who cares about objects more than human beings.

"Okay, you can hold it," I said, and soon her fingers roamed through my jewelry box once again, lifting up this and that and murmuring, "Beauty-full." I told myself there'd be plenty of time, after they all moved out, to care about objects more than human beings.

Though I learned to put up with messiness, which is, after all, a temporary condition, I didn't have to deal with much permanent damage because, outside of a stain here and there and an unremovable mark on an antique desk, our house came through the onslaught of the Alexander Five with most of its walls, floors, and furnishings intact. I can't say how I'd have handled chips on my beautiful flowered dishes or water marks on my handsome dining-room table, but I like to think I'd have risen to the challenge. Indeed, I am proud to report that during the time that our extended family was living here I never once was tempted (well, I never was *significantly* tempted) to turn into one of those people whom I recently read about in *The New York Times*.

These are the kind of people who—whenever they entertain—impose strict party rules to protect their stuff, brazenly choosing undamaged over hospitable. Many of them, with their pale-colored rugs and expensive, fragile fabrics, do not allow red wine to be served in their homes, and one of them prohibits any food that's red or brown, including not only red wine but beets and chocolate. Others, protective of their recently refinished floors, stop guests at the door and ask them to take off their shoes, sometimes reshodding their feet in white paper booties or embroidered Chinese slippers. And perhaps the most drastic example of what the *Times* nicely characterized as Extreme Hosting is the couple who, afraid of winding up with water marks on their wood furniture, a fear that I can definitely relate to, cover every wood surface in their place—before a party—with plastic wrap!

The *Times* describes a host who replied to a guest's request for red wine by asking for a blank check to cover all damages, noting that "this maneuver is not for beginners." It is somehow comforting to know that, no matter how dire the threats to my floors or my velvets, I never attempted to master this maneuver.

When I say I'm a better person, even though I'm basically not a different person, I mean I now know I can override my nature and my needs in the higher interests of familial harmony. I mean I now know that I actually can, in the interests of getting along with my children and theirs, live for a while—indeed, for quite a long while—with unpredictability and messiness, and do so without a psychotic break or even much subterranean resentment. The fact that since they've left I have reverted to all of my pre-Alexander Five habits suggests that I am still the person I was. But this doesn't detract from the fact that lurking deep deep down inside me is the capacity to be—should it happen to be demanded of me—flexible.

Another aspect of this newly uncovered flexibility is my ability—*was* my ability while they were living here—to live with a considerable lack of privacy. For though Marla and Alexander were always careful not to invade my personal space, little O showed no such inhibitions. Weekends and evenings, vacation days and sick days, whenever I was at home and she was around, there was no place I went that she didn't feel free to follow, singing songs and asking questions and offering various tidbits of information and talking talking talking talking talking.

"Are Louie Armstrong and Lance Armstrong brothers?"

"Isaac and ice cream and iPod all start with 'I.'"

"Dragons are make-believe, but giants aren't."

"I don't want Charlotte [of *Charlotte's Web*] to die, I'm allergic to plums, and Ethan's my boyfriend but I'm not going to marry him."

She also, out of the blue, unleashed a stream of naughty words, explaining to me when I expressed some surprise, "My mommy got mad and said those words, but then she said she was giving herself a Time Out."

When I was at my computer, having told O that I needed to finish some serious work, she would stand by my desk asking, "When will you stop being serious?" When I was in the bathroom—there are four of them in our house—she would sit down on the floor inquiring, "When is it my turn—I want to use *your* potty." Whenever I answered the telephone, she would hover at my side, wondering who I was talking to and what I was talking about and how long it was going to be before I hung up. And when I was in my bedroom, stretched out on my bed and reading, or trying to read, a novel, she would stretch herself out beside me and ask, as she had asked a hundred times before, "How old are you, JuJu? Tell me—I won't tell anyone."

I announce my age every decade or so in the titles of my books, the last title being *I'm Too Young to Be Seventy,* and I feel no obligation to go public with further details, though I certainly don't conceal my age from my friends. I conceal it from O, however, because she'd probably save up her money and announce it in a full-page ad in the *Post,* responding instead to her wheedling, demanding, relentless pursuit of the truth in three different ways: I'm not telling you. I'm a hundred and nine years old. And—this answer, I'm pleased to say, drives her crazy—I'm five feet, five and three quarter inches tall.

"JuJu," she'll growl, "I'm asking how old you are, not how tall you are."

To which I reply, driving her even crazier, "I'm five feet, five and three quarter inches tall."

Showering, bathing, exercising, sleeping, tweezing my eyebrows, shaving my legs, putting on makeup, polishing my nails, I rarely—if Olivia was anywhere on the premises—was alone. And although I perhaps need more time for myself than many people do, although I could be quite happy spending a day, maybe even two, without human company or a phone conversation, and although hanging out with O required every ounce of my energy and attention, I wouldn't, looking back, relinquish one moment of it.

Because she's so interesting. Because she's so much fun. Because she's both bossy and sensitive, silly and smart. And because the way she looks at the world—so thoroughly, so thoughtfully, so questioningly, so full of amazement and joy—keeps prompting me to open my eyes and notice (as Lance's brother Louie would have it) that it is—it is indeed—a wonderful world.

I know that I also took pleasure in my own three children when they were growing up. They delighted me and they certainly opened my eyes. But I often felt squeezed in a vise by all the constant, concurrent demands of motherhood and marriage and a career. On any given day, as I sped from car-pool duties to marketing, wrote for three or four hours before I picked up the boys to buy jeans or get them their shots, I would have throttled anyone who suggested that I stop and smell the roses. And while I still believe that being a mother is a lot harder for women today, I wouldn't want anyone thinking that being a mother back in my day was all that easy.

But if motherhood is difficult, being a grandmother is a whole other deal, filling our hearts with uncomplicated happiness and our wallets with shameless numbers of photographs. In our relationship with our grandchildren there are fewer obligations and more enjoyment, fewer expectations and more acceptance, fewer lessons and a lot more laughter, fewer vegetables and more dessert. It's delicious being a grandparent. I am loving being a grandparent. And with Milton beside me, wholeheartedly loving it, too, our grandparent identities, our Papa and JuJu identities, are shaping the way we are currently living our lives.

We're becoming less ambitious—we're not reaching so high or pushing so damn hard. We're still in the game, but we don't have to run every race. And if we're now moving at a slower pace, we are (usually) sturdy enough to keep up with our grandchildren. We still—let me pause to knock on wood—have the energy. And we now have the time.

We have time to fly to Denver to hang out with Bryce and Miranda. We have time to fly to New York to go to the playground with Nathaniel and Benjamin. We have time to watch *Elmo* with Isaac and to tickle Toby's toes and to color in the coloring book with Olivia. We have time to slow down, and stop, and smell the roses.

Being a grandparent, once described as "parenthood one step removed," turns out to be, to be more precise about it, parenthood one *blissful* step removed.

Even when our youngest son, his wife, their baby, their toddler, and their five-year-old were living here with us for ninety days.

Especially when our youngest son, his wife, their baby, their toddler, and their five-year-old were living here with us for ninety wonderful, marvelous, unforgettable days.